BLACKS IN BONDAGE

BLACKS IN BONDAGE
Letters of American Slaves

edited by
Robert S. Starobin
State University of New York, Binghamton

with a new foreword by
Ira Berlin
University of Maryland

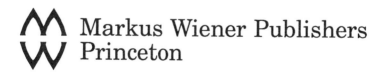 Markus Wiener Publishers
Princeton

First Markus Wiener Publishers Edition 1988
Second Edition 1994

For information write to Markus Wiener Publishers,
114 Jefferson Road, Princeton, NJ 08540

Library of Congress Cataloging-in-Publication Data

Blacks in bondage: letters of American slaves/edited by
    Robert S. Starobin; with a new foreword by Ira Berlin.
    Reprint. Originally published: New York:
New Viewpoints, 1974. With new foreword.
    Bibliography
    ISBN 0-910129-87-8 (pbk.)
    1. Slaves—United States—Correspondence.
    2. Slavery—United States. I. Starobin, Robert S.
E444.B62   1987   87-33408
973'.0496—dc19   CIP

Cover Design by Cheryl Mirkin

Printed in the United States of America

Blacks in Bondage:
Letters of American Slaves—An Appreciation

Robert S. Starobin took his life in 1971. He was thirty-one years old, and, if one can ever be too young to die, Robert Starobin was too young. A revolutionary, a scholar, a teacher, a husband, and a father—his short time was filled with accomplishment and with promise of still greater accomplishment. There might have been so much more.

Robert Starobin careened through life, throttle wide open, pedal jammed to the floor, accelerating faster and faster at each turn. He was a leader of the Free Speech Movement at Berkeley in the early sixties, an active participant in the anti-war movement at Wisconsin later in the decade, and, at the time of his death, a supporter of the Black Panther party. His commitment to change—radical change, revolutionary change—crested when most other Americans were retreating from the full implications of the social transformation these movements had wrought. The movements themselves had fallen into disarray. The tension was great, and for Starobin ultimately too great.

Starobin was a scholar as well as a revolutionary. By the time of his death, he had published two books, and each had gained recognition as a significant contribution to his chosen field of study, the history of the slave South. *Industrial Slavery in the Old South* (1970) surveyed the use of slaves in manufacturing, transportation, and mining during the late antebellum period. Historians are loath to use the word definitive, but Starobin's history of industrial slavery was as close to being definitive as any. He had visited every major Southern archive and most of the minor ones, and wrung their collections dry. His prodigious energy and considerable skill as a researcher made him something of a legend within the fraternity of Southern historians and won the admiration even of those who disdained his Marxist approach. But *Industrial Slavery* was notable for more than its thoroughness or its ideological perspective. By demonstrating that slaveowners were moving their "peculiar" labor force into the most advanced sector of the economy, Starobin's work raised important questions about the character of the slaveholding class and silenced the notion that slavery would have died a natural death without the march of the Union army.

Starobin also edited a documentary history of the Denmark Vesey conspiracy of 1822 (1970). Vesey, a Charleston free black, had united the city's slave artisans with the field hands of the adjacent rice plantations in the largest slave conspiracy in American history. The plot was discovered on the eve of the planned revolt, and Vesey and his chief lieutenants were tried and executed. Starobin wove the rich record of the trial and related correspondence into a documentary history that remains the best account of the Vesey conspiracy.

Starobin's choice of subject and genre suggested his desire to link his commitment to social revolution with the study of the revolutionary past. Like many young scholar-activists, Starobin had come to believe that understanding the nature of slavery, the character of Afro-American culture, and a host of related questions was essential to a successful resolution of the racial crisis of the day. As the record of the Vesey conspiracy revealed, few methods seemed as useful to this project as the slaves' own words. Writing a documentary history of slavery offered a means to unite politics and history, making the revolution and making a living.

It was precisely these linkages which sent Starobin back to the sources. During his many trips to the archives, Starobin uncovered a substantial number—perhaps as many as several hundred—letters written by slaves. Many of them were from "privileged" bondsmen and women—house servants, artisans, and drivers. Their letters, written to powerful white men and women, were almost always carefully crafted for obvious purposes. But others were written by field hands, to friends and relatives of like status. And even the letters of the most well-placed slaves, written for the most transparent of reasons, told much about the slaves' world.

In the 1960s, such sources were largely unknown to students of black life. Starobin's own mentor, the distinguished historian of slavery Kenneth M. Stampp, had prefaced his history of slavery in the American South with a reminder that "since there are few reliable records of what went on in the minds of slaves, one can only infer their thoughts and feelings from their behavior, that of their masters, and the logic of their situation." Other scholars concurred. Writing in a pioneer volume on the black studies movement, Nathan Hare, a young sociologist, reluctantly agreed with Stampp, ruefully observing that "if a black historian is going to publish in one of the learned journals, especially if he's going to publish on the slavery era, he is placed in the very ludicrous and unenviable position of having to footnote white slave masters or the scholarly representatives of that era."

Blacks in Bondage: Letters of American Slaves contradicted this conventional wisdom and placed the history of slavery on a new footing. It affirmed Starobin's belief that the history of slavery could be written from the perspective of the slaves—rather than those who owned them, those who observed them, or even those who wanted to free them. Here were documents that spoke to the slaves' understanding of slavery—not their numbers or value, as did censuses or tax lists; not their work patterns, as did plantation ledgers and travelers accounts; not their crimes, as did court records and newspapers. Such letters also offered real advantages over other sources of direct testimony by blacks, such as the reminiscences of former slaves collected by the WPA, which spoke of slavery nearly a lifetime after it had ended, or even contemporary autobiographies, written partly as abolitionist propaganda and partly as object lessons in the exemplary life. *Blacks in Bondage* provided new entry into the slaves' world.

Starobin's collection had another equally important historiographic purpose. While pointing to the availability of the slaves' own words, he also alerted scholars to the fact that every source—whatever its origin—had its own biases and limitations. The slaves' letters were a corrective to those of the slave owners, but they too were written with an agenda. That agenda was complex, having to do with each author's place within the slave community, as well as his or her own goals. The letters of slaves, Starobin cautioned, had to be read with extreme care: "they are loaded with subtleties of meaning, irony, double entendres, and outright put-ons." Like the sources of slavery that derived from free whites, those derived from enslaved blacks had to be understood in their context.

As it turns out, *Blacks in Bondage* served both of Starobin's purposes. It made available some one hundred letters written by blacks during or immediately after slavery, while suggesting how they could best be understood. These letters immediately became an indispensable source to historians of slave life. The publication of *Blacks in Bondage* also set historians looking for other such sources. In the years that followed, scholars unearthed other direct testimony about slavery by slaves themselves. Today, no one would think of writing the history of slavery without it.

Ira Berlin
University of Maryland
December 1987

ACKNOWLEDGMENTS

GRATEFUL ACKNOWLEDGMENT IS made to the following organizations and individuals for permission to quote from their materials:

The University of North Carolina Library, for selections from the Pettigrew Family Papers, the DeRosset Family Papers, and the Ernest Haywood Collection, all from the Southern Historical Collection.

The Alabama State Department of Archives and History, for a selection from the Tait Family Papers.

The University of Virginia Library, for selections from the Grinnan Papers.

The Tulane University Library, for selections from the Charles Colcock Jones Papers and the John McDonogh Papers, from the Special Collections Division.

The Historical Society of Pennsylvania, for selections from the Pennsylvania Abolition Society Papers.

The North Carolina State Archives, for selections from the James Boon Papers.

The New-York Historical Society, for a selection from the Miscellaneous Collection.

The Duke University Library, for selections from the David Campbell Papers, the Joseph Long Papers, the Richard B. Riddick Papers, and the Neill Brown Papers.

ACKNOWLEDGMENTS

The University of Mississippi, for selections from the Andrew Brown Correspondence File, Learned Collection, Lumber Archives.

The Maryland Historical Society, for selections from the Otho Holland Williams Papers.

The Library of Congress, for selections from the American Colonization Society Papers.

We wish to plead our own cause. Too long have others spoken for us.

—*Opening editorial statement,* Freedom's Journal, *New York, March 16, 1827*

The new Negro shall not be deceived. The new Negro refuses to take advice from anyone who has not felt with him, and suffered with him. We have suffered for three hundred years; therefore, we feel that the time has come when only those who have suffered with us can interpret our feelings and our spirit. It takes the slaves to interpret the feelings of the slave; it takes the unfortunate man to interpret the spirit of his unfortunate brother; and so it takes the suffering Negro to interpret the spirit of his comrade.

—*Marcus Garvey,* Philosophy and Opinions (*1932*)

If a black historian is going to publish in one of the learned journals, especially if he's going to publish on the slavery era, he is placed in the very ludicrous and unenviable position of having to footnote white slave masters or the scholarly representatives of that era. The blacks weren't even allowed to learn to read and write, let alone write history in those days . . . yet this is the era from which we have to get our footnotes and documentation. So, we don't feel that that history is valid or that any history based on that [white] documentation is valid. We are going to have to declare it all void and to start the writing of that history all over again. . . .

—*Nathan Hare,* Black Studies in the University (*1969*)

PREFACE

A GENERATION AGO, W. E. B. DuBois chided historians for writing "the record of kings and gentlemen ad nauseum and in stupid detail. . . . Of the common run of human beings . . . and particularly of the . . . working group," he noted, "the world has saved all too little of authentic record and tried to forget or ignore even the little saved." [1] A few years earlier, scholars had been reminded that "any history of slavery must be written in large part from the standpoint of the slave." [2] Despite these longstanding pleas for an approach to black history from the point of view of the blacks, historians have only just begun to develop the sources, methods, and perspective that will enable them to write black history from a new viewpoint. I hope that this collection of documents will contribute to the growing body of literature on slavery, so that the daily life of bondsmen can someday be depicted "from the bottom up."

Historians of slavery frequently despair of ever finding adequate sources written by slaves themselves. "Since there are few reliable records of what went on in the minds of slaves," wrote Kenneth M. Stampp in 1956, "one can only infer their thoughts and feelings from their behavior, that of their masters, and the logic of their situation." [3] Similarly, Stanley Elkins constructed his study of slavery [4] around a loose analogy between Southern plantations and German concentration camps. Elkins' findings

xv

were, however, based almost entirely on secondary accounts. As recently as 1967, George Fredrickson and Christopher Lasch stated bluntly that slavery was "an unrecorded experience, except from the masters' point of view." Since "adequate records of personal slave response simply do not exist," they maintained, it is "tempting to resort to" and "indeed almost impossible to avoid" comparing bondage with other "total institutions" like prisons. "Those who condemn analogies, pretending to argue from documentary evidence alone," they warned, "delude themselves." [5]

Without dismissing the usefulness of some analogies, I should like to suggest that documents written or articulated by slaves or freedmen themselves do in fact exist in sufficient quantity for the purposes of analysis. This material consists of a rich body of folklore, spirituals, work songs, tales, poetry, oral traditions, dances, music, religious customs, and crafts. These sources are still being uncovered, and they are being analyzed by such scholars as Sterling Stuckey, Robert Ascher, and Robert Farris Thompson.[6]

Moreover, sources exist pertaining to resistance to bondage, including slave petitions for freedom to state legislatures, letters to antislavery organizations from slaves seeking assistance, and letters from fugitive slaves to black friends, former masters, or Underground Railroad agents. There are, in addition, written communications among slave rebels, letters and testimony by Negro informers against conspiracies, voluntary or forced confessions by slave rebels implicated in insurrections and plots, letters to the American Colonization Society from slaves seeking to return to Africa, letters from the Liberian settlers to relatives and former masters, and the well-known fugitive-slave narratives. These letters, stories, and reminiscences still await careful analytical treatment, though some work with narrative materials has been done by Gilbert Osofsky and Julius Lester.[7]

Finally, there is a fascinating correspondence—amounting to a few hundred letters—which reveals the daily life and inner thoughts of slaves themselves. These sources include letters to their masters and mistresses from slave drivers, managers, house servants, artisans, hirelings, and field hands. This correspondence also comprises several letters from one slave to another, most interestingly between those bondsmen who were married and between slaves about to be sold or already caught up in the interstate slave traffic. Documents relating to the plantation routine and black resistance, written or articulated by slaves themselves, form the bulk of the materials in this book. Altogether they comprise a magnificent body of primary documents which have remained virtually unexplored and unanalyzed.

Compared to those written by the slaves themselves, the traditional sources available for the study of slavery are more familiar and extensive. Scholars customarily have consulted plantation journals, court records, census schedules, and travelers' accounts, all of which yield valuable information about servitude. Plantation day books contain listings on the work routine, the provision of food and clothing, and the problem of sickness and medical care, as well as on such slave behavior as fighting, stealing, and running away. Court records reveal the nature of punishments for slave miscreants and the temper of "Southern justice." Census schedules contain statistical data about Southern society and can, for example, provide information on the transfer of slaves from the Upper South to newer regions, and on the growth rate of the black population. In short, it is possible to gain from standard sources considerable insight into the social structure of the Old South.

Despite these assets, the traditional records have many serious limitations. Plantation journals deal mainly with the masters' farming operations and only rarely with the motivations of the slaves. Government records were often so haphazardly taken that they are not always reliable, and court records do not always acknowledge the gulf between the language of state codes and their application. Most travelers simply were not equipped to evaluate what they encountered, and they often had strong moral convictions which tended to vitiate the accuracy of their observations. Except for travelers like Frederick Law Olmsted,

PREFACE

visitors saw only limited, well-traveled areas of the South, often so rapidly that they hardly had time to digest their impressions.

The basic problem with these traditional sources, however, is that they present slavery entirely from the white man's point of view. Such evidence generally depicts black people more as whites (even sympathetic whites) wanted or imagined them to be than as they actually were. The standard sources tell more about the mentality of masters than about the character of their chattels. Indeed, by their very nature they depict slavery more from the top down than from the bottom up.

Fugitive-slave narratives and freedman reminiscences are valuable sources which deserve to be considered as a literary genre in their own right. These autobiographies vividly recall the hardships of plantation life, the rigors of the domestic slave trade, the complex and often tragic relationship between bondsmen and their masters, and the pervasive brutality of the slave system.[8] The accounts also reveal the personal, family, and religious lives of slaves, as well as the circumstances which made some blacks more rebellious than others and compelled some bondsmen to escape. Thus the narratives of Frederick Douglass, William Wells Brown, Henry Bibb, and Solomon Northrup are, among many others, masterpieces of self-expression and social analysis. Such autobiographies were written, it is true, by the most gifted, privileged, and successfully rebellious bondsmen, but this does not mean that such slaves were not also exceptionally perceptive. Moreover, the Federal Writers' Project and Fisk University collections of interviews, which have been assembled and analyzed by Julius Lester and George Rawick, firmly establish the possibilities for an intriguing study of oral-tradition personal histories.[9] For these reasons, therefore, the narratives and recollections are very useful documents through which to explore the attitudes of fugitive and manumitted slaves.

To be sure, the slave narratives must be treated with more caution than they usually have been, and for several reasons only some of them are helpful for a study of bondage from the black man's viewpoint. Since most of the accounts were written many years after successful escapes, the experiences of freedom almost inevitably distorted the remembrances of servitude. Many of the fugitives were illiterate (but not inarticulate), and antislavery publicists often helped with their writing and narration. In the 1840's and 1850's, when the narratives became a popular form of literature as well as abolitionist propaganda "calculated to exert a very wide influence on public opinion," many of the narratives were rewritten to conform to the literary standards of the time, and tended to become romanticized and moralistic to suit the tastes of Northern and British readers. Also, abolitionists thought that if the narratives were published in the language of the ex-slaves, with its own rules of grammar and rhetoric, they would provide proslavery apologists with further arguments for black inferiority; the slaves' stories were thus presented in a manner that could not be criticized, resulting in the loss of much of their original content and spirit.[10]

Similarly, the recollections of the freedmen, such as those in B. A. Botkin's *Lay My Burden Down*, the Federal Writers' Project's *Negro in Virginia*, and Julius Lester's *To Be a Slave*, were recorded so long after slavery that post–Civil War experiences tended to affect antebellum ones, and specific events were not always accurately remembered. On the other hand, unlike the abolitionists, the Federal Writers' Project interviewers were interested in preserving the speech patterns and language of ex-slaves. Therefore, even though slave reminiscences deserve close attention, they should be supplemented with slave letters.[11]

Compared with the traditional sources, the slave correspondence has several distinct advantages. Unlike the slave narratives, most slave letters were written while the slaves were still in bondage in the South; consequently, lapses of memory so characteristic of the recollections are absent. The emotional trauma which accompanied and followed escapes is minimized in the correspondence between slaves and their masters. Abolitionist ghostwriting is, of course, absent, since the letters were actually written or dictated by slaves. The letters reflect slaves' thoughts, emotions, and feelings while still in bondage. They preserve the words, spelling, grammar, punctuation, and alliteration actually used by blacks. (The chirography was often artistic, even if the orthography was frequently unintelligible.)

The letters reveal also the drive for and extent of literacy in the slave community, despite regulations against education and writing. Indeed, the whole question of literacy must be reevaluated from the slaves' perspective and in the light of whom the slaves were addressing. Whether the letters were intended for whites or blacks, for public or private reading, must be taken into account. To impose the white man's standards of literacy on the enslaved is both irrelevant and arrogant, and to measure them by that standard often masks the ability of barely literate bondsmen to speak their mind. In short, I believe that the letters are one of the best tools historians may find for an understanding of slavery from the black man's perspective.

On the other hand, the slave letters do present some problems. A few, but not many, were dictated to an amanuensis who supposedly transcribed the slave's thoughts and words exactly as they were spoken and intended. The feelings of the white transcriber may nonetheless have affected the expression of the slave author and placed the black under subtle forms of duress. Since slaves were writing to whites or were aware that whites might intercept letters to blacks, not all portions of the letters should be accepted literally. Slaves were conscious of the need to deceive for purposes of survival, not only when they communicated with each other, but also—and especially—when they addressed their masters. Thus the letters have to be read with extreme care, for they are loaded with subtleties of meaning, irony, double entendres, and outright put-ons. In addition, many of the letters were written by privileged bondsmen, those house servants, drivers, and artisans who made up an elite group of perhaps 5 or 10 percent of the total slave population. These slaves usually lived in the cities or in the "big house" of the largest plantations, in environments which were not representative of the average slave's milieu. They were not only beholdened to whites for their special status, but—unlike field hands who might find succor in the anonymity of the slave quarter—were usually under constant white supervision. Although most of the slave letters come from the hands of such bondsmen, a few letters written by ordinary slaves have come to light. These precious documents must be used intensively, for the mass of evidence presented herein pertains to the upper crust of slave society.

Fortunately, some pioneering methodology has already been developed which can facilitate the use of the slave letters. Edward P. Thompson's *The Making of the English Working Class* (1964), Eric Hobsbawm's *Primitive Rebels* (1959), and George Rudé's *The Crowd in History* (1964) are but three examples of recent Marxist scholarship on the politics and culture of the European working class, peasantry, and "mobs." Jesse Lemisch has been studying the political attitudes of merchant seamen during the American Revolution; Ira Berlin has been investigating the free blacks in the antebellum South; Herbert Gutman has been uncovering materials on workers—black and white—in the late-nineteenth-century United States.[12] These scholars have been tapping hitherto unused sources such as police reports, church records, tax and voting rolls, as well as the workers' own diaries, letters, and newspapers. More important, they have been approaching these sources specifically from the workers' and peasants' point of view. They suggest how the meager documentation of working-class culture can be made to speak aloud. Similarly, anthropologists, folklorists, and African historians have long been developing techniques for analyzing the oral traditions of largely nonliterate peoples. Jan Vansina's *Oral Tradition* is a pioneering work in the African field, while Sterling Stuckey—by examining black tales, spirituals, and folksongs—has been "trying to get 'inside' slaves to discover what they thought about their condition." [13] Given the new sources and methodology, therefore, is it not time for young scholars—in one black man's words—"to start the writing of history all over again"?

Throughout the book I have kept the original spelling and punctuation of the letters. I have indicated with brackets where words are missing because of deterioration or illegibility. Finally, I have also attempted to determine who wrote the document—

the slave or an amanuensis—and, where possible, have indicated that in the notes.

For assistance in the preparation of this book, I would like to express my indebtedness to the archival staffs of the University of North Carolina Library, Duke University Library, the University of Virginia Library, the Library of Congress, and Tulane University Library. Sarah Diamant and Bo Nelson of Ithaca, New York, and Ivan Dee, former editor of Quadrangle Books, was also helpful. A postdoctoral research fellowship for 1969–1970 from the Cornell Society for the Humanities enabled me to spend several months completing a manuscript begun four years ago. I alone, of course, am responsible for whatever errors remain.

R. S.

Binghamton, New York
September 1970

CONTENTS

Contents

PART
ONE

The Black Elite Report on Slave Life

norfolk   november 17 1811

Dear Madam   your pore old survint Tristram takes the liberty of saying Howdy too you

God bless

—from the John H. Cocke Papers

Harrodsburg, Kentucky
Oct. 15th 1834

Miss Louisa Bethley

I have got greatly disappointed in my expectations on next Saturday. I will be compelled to disappoint you at that time but I regret it very much. Master says I must put it off a little longer, until he can see farther into the matter. he says probably Mr. Birney may break up house keeping or something of the kind and he dont know what may become of you, for that reason we must defer it a little longer. I will come up and see you shortly and then we will make some arrangements about it. it is with great reluctance that I put it off any longer, but I am compelled to do it owing to the circumstances I have related. I shall remain your affectionate lover until death.

Milo Thompson

—Quoted in Dwight L. Dumond, ed.,
Letters of James Gillespie Birney (*1938*)

*P*ractically all the colonies founded by the European powers in the New World from the sixteenth through the eighteenth century were heavily dependent upon slave labor. Without the forced work of millions of Indians and Africans, the development of plantations, mines, and other enterprises would not have been feasible in such countries as Portuguese Brazil, Spanish Cuba, French Saint-Domingue, Dutch Surinam, and the British West Indies. By the nineteenth century, the slave system was also firmly entrenched in the economic, political, and social structure of the southern regions of the United States, where several million bondsmen helped build what soon would become one of the world's most powerful nations.

In 1860 the population of the fifteen slave states included 8 million whites, 4 million black slaves, and 250,000 free blacks. Of the whites, about 1 million lived in desperate poverty on marginal lands. The great majority, about 5 million, were small yeoman farmers or petty tradesmen and artisans. Therefore, only 385,000 white families, or some 2 million persons, had a proprietary interest in slaves. About 88 percent of these slaveholders were farmers who owned but one or two blacks and a few hundred acres of good land. The remaining 12 percent of the slaveowners, the planter class, owned more than twenty slaves each, employed overseers, and held the best Southern lands. Fewer than 3,000 planters held more than one hundred bondsmen each. Thus the typical slaveholder was a farmer, but the planters controlled more than half of the slave population.

Most of the 4 million slaves worked on plantations, concentrated in the so-called Tidewater, Piedmont, Black Belt, and Delta regions. Plantation slaves produced practically all of the South's cotton, rice, sugar, hemp, and tobacco. Slaves also raised corn, wheat, vegetables, and cattle, and engaged in other agricultural work. By the 1850's about 200,000 bondsmen also worked in industrial enterprises located in rural, small-town, or urban settings. These industries included manufacturing, mining, lumbering, turpentining, fishing, crop processing, construction, and operating transportation facilities. Most industrial slaves were owned outright by their employers; others were hired by the day, month, season, or year. In the South's eight leading cities there were about 70,000 urban slaves, most of whom were domestic servants or service tradesmen. Others were skilled craftsmen or industrially employed. Of course, large plantations usually had a number of household servants and slave artisans to make the estate self-sufficient and the master as comfortable as possible.

Most of the 250,000 free blacks were farm workers or small landowners living in the Upper South. Others lived in Southern cities and towns, where they worked as service tradesmen, domestic servants, or craftsmen. As their numbers increased and as slavery consolidated, free blacks came to be regarded as an economic and political threat. Were they not, reasoned Southerners, a bad example for slaves? Might they not provide leadership for abolitionist or insurrectionary movements? Consequently, the position of the free black in Southern society was increasingly that of the pariah.

Slavery was integral to the economic growth of the South as well as the nation. The fantastic increase in slave-grown cotton, sugar, and rice was largely responsible for Southern prosperity. And these Southern crops contributed to national economic growth from 1815 to 1861, especially since cotton remained the leading export of the United States until the 1850's.

Because slave-owning planters dominated the staple-export sector of the American economy, they enjoyed enormous wealth, prestige, and power. A tradition of political leadership, the ideology of agrarianism, and their class hegemony further solidified the dominance of planters. Slavery was profitable for most plantations, farms, and industries, and slave labor was comparatively cheaper than the available free labor. Class antagonisms among Southern whites tended to be subsumed by divisions along racial lines. Fear of manumission, racial equality, miscegenation, and slave rebellion—all of which were strengthened by the proslavery ideology propagated by masters—convinced most Southern whites that slavery was a racial necessity as well as the easiest way to wealth and power. (Although most Northern whites also hated blacks, especially the free blacks, they ultimately came to view slavery as a greater and more immediate threat to the free-labor system.)

"Unrelieved horror and vicious cruelty" characterized the day-to-day existence of most slaves. The workday lasted from before sunup to after sundown. Labor in the fields or factories was arduous and exhausting. Masters kept food, clothing, and shelter to the bare minimum for a subsistence standard of living. High morbidity and mortality rates, as well as endemic and epidemic diseases for which medical care was inadequate, resulted from poor working and living conditions. Masters, overseers, and foremen often drove their blacks brutally to obtain maximum production and profits. To ensure steady work, most slave-owners combined punishments with more subtle incentives—"overwork" pay, permission to visit another plantation, a new suit of clothes—but whipping, shackling, and other brutal punishments were common.

Bondage severely restricted the mobility, religion, family life, and other personal rights of the slaves. Slave codes legally transformed people into property; the proslavery ideology held that blacks were naturally inferior to whites. Slave-owners consciously attempted to destroy African culture, religion, family forms, and any sense of personal identity, by force or through suffocating paternalism. To eliminate African religions, masters inculcated slaves with conservative Christian principles and forbade independent black religious gatherings. The African family structure (in both its matrifocal and patrifocal forms) was strained by the forced separation of slave families and by the brutalization of slave fathers and mothers. Thus did the slave system attempt to obliterate the black's human dignity.

Still, whites were never able to strip blacks of their distinctive culture. Instead, in the shadow of the plantation house and in the back alleys of Southern cities, the heritage of Africa and the conditions of bondage blended into a new, Afro-American culture. Little is known about slavery during the formative years of the development of Afro-American culture—the seventeenth and eighteenth centuries. Indeed, little is known

[7]

about the distinctive values and mores of this culture as reflected in, for example, slave family life, child rearing patterns, and standards of personal relations during the nineteenth century. But, as the rich legacy of black folklore and black music prove, such a culture did exist.

CHAPTER ONE

Drivers and Managers

O N SMALL FARMS, masters could manage their own slaves, but on plantations it was necessary to employ an overseer and to make the estate as self-sufficient as possible. Since white managers were scarce and expensive in the Old South, a slave known as a driver or foreman sometimes worked under the overseer or master to supervise and discipline the field hands. Drivers had great responsibilities, superior privileges, and awesome disciplinary powers. Some foremen had virtually complete control of the plantation when the master or overseer was absent. In this respect, drivers helped make the plantation system a self-sufficient agricultural unit and acted as agents of accommodation for the field workers.

The drivers' position between owners and slaves placed them in a difficult role. In effect, the foremen were compelled to control and discipline their fellow bondsmen for the benefit of their masters in order to maintain order on the estate. Sometimes drivers punished slaves more severely than whites did; their ambiguous position thus could express itself in vicious cruelty. But most drivers bent the other way, and they often used their position to protect the slaves and ease the burden of bondage. Drivers could also become, albeit rarely, leaders of escape attempts and resistance movements, as was sometimes evident during the Civil War.

Because many foremen were literate, their reports to their masters survive, giving some suggestion of the dilemmas they faced, as well as the plantation routines they directed.

One master who used black overseers was William S. Pettigrew, of North Carolina. Pettigrew was born in 1818 and schooled in law at the University of North Carolina. He forsook a legal practice and, after 1838, lived at his two plantations—Magnolia and nearby Belgrade—in Tyrrell County. Each plantation was worked by about forty slaves, including fifteen men, fifteen women, and their children, who farmed a variety of grain crops and tobacco. From June to October every year in the 1850's, Pettigrew (who was a bachelor) vacationed at the Virginia mineral springs; in 1857–1858 he was absent from home for almost a whole year. Rather than use white overseers whom he found to be "of harsh, unyielding tempers," in his absence he entrusted the management of his plantations entirely to his two black overseers, Moses and Henry, whom he instructed by letter. The slaves in turn made weekly reports to their master by means of letters dictated through Malachi White, a neighboring white farmer. Though this white farmer and other friends of Pettigrew seem to have been in the vicinity of his estates, the intriguing thing about the arrangements is that the two black overseers were virtually in complete charge of the plantation operations, so that at Pettigrew's places there was no white overseer or master present for many months of the year.

The use of black foremen did not seem to have hindered the profitability of Pettigrew's plantations, but it did cause some special problems. To discipline his slaves and maintain production, Pettigrew tried to instill a sort of plantation pride in his black overseers and other hands. "Will you remember me kindly to the people and say to them that I hope they are conducting themselves well," the master urged the black overseers again and again. "They should do so, and I hope [they] will. Their good conduct will be very gratifying to me and will add greatly to their credit and to the good name of their home." Moses and Henry, for their part, seemed to absorb these themes, but it is interest-

ing to note how they used them to win special privileges for
themselves and their people.

William Pettigrew, on a holiday, writes Moses about the
overseers' responsibility to "your people."

Healing Springs, Bath C. Va.
June 24, 1856

Moses:

Thinking you would be glad to hear from me, I
have concluded to write you a few lines and will
enclose them to Mr. White who will read them to you.
I have frequently thought of you since having left
home, and have been anxious that your business
might go on well & that the health of your people
might continue good. Should any of them be sick, be
sure not to neglect them. You must do all in your
power to promote the welfare and credit of Belgrade
during my absence. The people promised me to be
industrious and obedient to you, you must remind
them of this promise should any of them be disposed
to forget it. I am anxious for your credit as well as my
own that all things should go on well & it would be
distressing & mortifying to me to hear the contrary
on my return home.

I have placed much reliance in your management, industry & honesty by thus leaving the plantation & all on it in your charge, nor have I any fear that
you will fall short of the confidence I have placed in
you. I suppose harvest has commenced and hope the
weather is such as to enable you to go on well with it.

You & Henry must endeavor to manage to the best advantage & occasionally you should talk together on the subject of what should be done. You must not be unfriendly to each other, as it would injure both places & yourselves, as well as myself. You may give them such time on Saturdays as you think proper. Mr. Johnston's health has been very much improved, I am glad to say. I am as usual well. Remember me to all the people— particularly to your Uncle Charles, Gillie & Lizzie, and believe me,

Your friend,
William S. Pettigrew [1]

I hope your Uncle Charles' feet are improving.

Moses and Henry report to Master Pettigrew.

July 5, 1856

I was happy to hear from master an am thankful to receve the lines witch master sent to me. I am in good health master an hope I shall remain in the same good health. I looked A long time to hear from master an was happy to receive the lines master sent. I hope that master is in the same good health an remain so. I take a great plesure of sending a few lines back to master an hope it may be a great comfort to master in reading of them. Dear master I commenced laying by the corn the 7 of June an got two hundred an seventy acres don before harvest. I commenced in the harvest the 25 of June an compleated it safe to the barn the 5 day of July.

The people has been faithful and dutiful to mee an to thare work and all have agreed together sence master left home. I am glad that tha have helt out so well in thare health all saving oncle charles and he has bin treated with the greates respects that could be required. nothing but his time moved him away from us.

The weat crop is only comon. the corn crop is very likely with good seasons an the help of god it is the best we have had for many years. as soon as master can make it convenant I should like to hear from him again. nothing more master at present only your servant   Moses [2]

July 5, 1856

Dear master. I return my respects to you. I was glad to hear from master. I have don all day in my power towards your benefit. I was glad to hear that master is in good health and Master Jonston also hoping it may remain so getting better. your corn is very much improved. I got through two hundred an 10 acres before harvest then spared all the hands to Moses at Belgrade. the hands has bin faithful to their duty an all has agreed well together. I wish to indulge all in my power. all is well at present master. Jack is in the same state as when you left. Arry is Well only distressed over her Brother Charles at Belgrade is ded. Ary an effy our respects to master wanting to see you very bad. Polly respects to master thanking him for my going to norfolk. I was sick two days after master left. I returned home to day fortnit lingered 2 or 3 days after my return in good health-at present, Mary is doing veary well at present so that she can do her work.

Your Servant   henry [3]

July 5, 1856

My dear master. I was glad to hear from you. I am in good health at present and I hope that theas few lines may find master in the same good health. I shall be glad to see master come home when maybe to his convenance. ef I never should see master no more I hope we shall meat in hevan.

Your servant   Lizzy [4]

The correspondence continues, revealing the ability of Moses and Henry to handle the complexities of the plantation routine and the close personal and familiar relations among the blacks on the plantations.

White Sulphur Springs,
Greenbrier Co. Va.
July 12, 1856

Moses:

I was very glad to receive your letter of the 5th of July, which came to hand yesterday. I left home, I presume, on Monday the 7th, and, having reached here on Friday afternoon, was but five days on the way, which was expeditious for so long a journey.

It grieved me sincerely to learn of the death of your poor Uncle Charles, although I could not say it surprised me, for I had for some time lost all hope of the ulcers on his legs & feet being cured, and thought it more than probable that we would never again meet on this earth. Yet I am sorry it so happened that I could not be at home at the time of his death, as it is ever a comfort to me to be present when my people make their departure for the land of Spirits. Our lot having been cast together here, & feeling that I am a friend & well wisher both for time & eternity to every one of them, it is my wish to see the last of them and to accompany their lifeless bodies to the grave, that final resting place for us all. You inform me that he had every attention; which I am satisfied of, & would be much pained if there was reason to think otherwise.

As you succed so well as a letter-writer, I must trouble you with writing more frequently. I wish you to send me a letter every other week & Henry every other week—which will enable me to hear from home *every week*. Perhaps Mr. White, who will be good enough to write for you, would prefer writing Saturdays; it will be immaterial to me on what day the letter is written so that one is sent every week. When it is Henry's time, he can ride out to Belgrade & Mr. White will write as he may request him. He will inform me of all that is worth reporting at Belgrade as well as Magnolia, and when you write, you will, in like manner, send me a report of what Henry says as to his affairs at Magnolia, as well as your own report.

After having read your letter myself, I handed it to my very good friend, Mr. Johnston, who read it with much interest & pleasure. He desired me to remember him particularly to you, & to say that he is very glad to hear your affairs are going on so well & that you owe it to *him* that I wrote you my last letter from the Healing Springs, as he requested me to write you. He hopes he may continue to receive good news from Belgrade; but he says, if he should hear bad reports he would have to write you himself. You see from this, Moses, how much interest Mr. Johnston takes in you and your people, and that should things take an unfavorable turn, in consequence of my long absence, not only would I be distressed, but he would also; and you & all your people would not only be disgraced in my estimation, but also in his. You must inform me where you are at work and how you get on with it, also as to the pea-field. I am glad to hear so favorably as to the corn, & that it will be laid by so early this year. The wheat you think is but common, which is the case all through this country.

You will give the people what rest and time may in your judgment appear proper. You know I wish time given them frequently at this season. Remember your gardens are to be made. Tell your Aunt Gilly & Lizzy that I hope they are well. I hope the Fall will be as healthy as could be expected for our climate. Remember me very kindly to all the people, both at Belgrade & Magnolia, and say to Henry that I will write him, in answer to his letter, the last of next week, which would be better than replying to both at this time. Say to him also that I am glad your Master Charles permitted him to purchase those hogs of Mr.

Alexander. Your Master Charles' letter came to hand yesterday. Give my love to your Master Charles, and believe me,

Your friend,
William S. Pettigrew [5]

P.S. Mr. Johnston's health is quite good and my own is as usual. You must remember me to your father & Aunt Airy.   W.S.P.

August the 2 1856

Dear master. I was glad to receve your letter wich came to hand the 30 of July.

My love to master an to master Jonston. all the people are well an wishes thare love to master. Molly is pleged with the rumatism. Mary child is sick witch I sent for the Doc today but he could not go for the present but will go as soon as he can. the corn has stood veary well at Magnolia, very which I would not believed how it has stood the drouth altho I was looking at it but we had a very good rain the first day of August wich has improved it very much. When we rote master befor we thought we would clean out the Bee tree canal but we saw master Charles and he told us to not clean it out yet an so we held holladays 3 days master an I went in the ten foot ditch to cleaning that out . the people has been veary well behaved since master left as could be expected master to me an has worked well. Nelson named to me that master wishes me to white wash Magnolia an Belgrade an I will white wash magnolia. master will pleas to wright

me whether nellson will white wash Belgrade or no
as I need him very bad among my small people. I
made 75 bags out of the twilling an it gave out. master
Polly wishes her love to master. she has bin sick
about a fortnight but is getting better. ef master will
pass all of my letters to master Jonston to read I
have some secrets to tell master but I will keep them
untill master comes home you will excuse this master

your Servant   henry

it is my wishes master ef you pleas sir for some carful
person to stay at Belgrade of nights when thoes work-
mons are there at work, ef master pleases

your servant
Moses [6]

August the 9 1856

Dear master. I receved no letter from you as I expected of the last week and I thought as it was your
wishes to hear from home every week I would wright
as tha might be missplaced. I take a delight in writing
to master my love an to master Jonston also an all the
people wishes thare love to master hoping master is
well. the people is all ingeneraly well some little com-
plant but nomore than could be expected for the
season. I am very sorry to inform master that the
crops on Belgrade is cut of so bad as I rote master
befor that it was fel short by the drouth but I think
master we shall be cut off one half at Belgrade by the
drouth. we are geting along with the work veary well.
since I sent master the last letter I have cleaned out

the main road an cleaned out all the leading ditches
except the poppolar nec ditches them I shall not clean
them now. the next gob will be the swamp mud master. the carpernters commenced geting of timba for
the quarter houses 1 augs tha have got all of the
timber but the sils an got them at the house I shall
start the saws on the 11 of august. your servant   Moses

the people is all wel behaved to me master

my love to master and to master Jonston. also. I have
not got through with my leading ditches an the others
I shall go to work on the coal the next I think. the
people is quite well master an veary well behaved an
wishes thare love to master hoping that master is well.
the crop at magnolia is veary good master.

your servant   henry [7]

June the 6 1857

Dear master. I was glad to hear from you hoping that
you are receeving good health an Mast. Johnson also.
I shall get through with the corn the 9 an shall get a
hundred an 30 acres of peas sown by the 10. it will
take after that 2 days to break the other peaground
an sowit. the 15 I want to go to laying by the corn as
master wishes to. sompthin on the subject of these
weavers I have enquired of gilly an lizzy an tha think
that tha canot give the instruction. thinking if thare
be any person to hire I have understood that miss
White is a veary good weaver undeed an can give
good instructions an master can inform me as he

wishes. I have not seen Mr. Sawyer since I heard from you to make the enquiry of him conserning the other partes of Mr. furlough, but will do so as soon as I see him. the people are all in good health an veary well behaved up to this time present. hoping that tha may hold out to the end

your servant   Moses [8]

As accouterments of their considerable responsibility, Pettigrew invested his overseers with special privileges, provided them with boots, greatcoats, and whips (all symbols of power on the plantation), kept the overseer position within one family group, and sent encouragement and gifts to other favorite slaves. "As far as I can, up to this time, form an opinon," Pettigrew once confided to his closest friend, "I think my people will, by assistance of the two negro men who have heretofore been over them (Henry at Magnolia, & Moses at Belgrade), work faithfully and conduct themselves well. It has been my effort, since my business has been so much increased, to stimulate the principal men to be faithful to me. They promise well, & appear to do so in good faith."

Healing Springs, Va.
July 6, 1857

Moses:

On Saturday, the 4th, I wrote Henry; but omitted to enclose to him a pass which I had promised, on leaving home, to send, granting permission to him & Polly Price to visit Mrs. Beasley in Plymouth during the holidays after corn is laid by & wheat thrashed. You will also find a pass for America, who will be permitted to go to the neighborhood of Plymouth at the same time, for the purpose of visiting her family. You will also find a pass for Affy to visit at Mr. Jordan Davenport's. These papers you can hand to Henry, who can deliver them to the persons for whom they are intended. Mr. White will please read them, in order that you may distinguish for whom they are intended. Henry will carry a mule & cart. As some money will be required, I enclose $5. for Henry, which you will hand him.

The people on both plantations will have the usual length of holiday after the corn is laid-by & wheat thrashed, which is about three days. I shall wish the outside of the houses whitewashed this summer.

The first work at which Henry will commence after the holidays are passed will be the cleaning out the old part of the Creek. This will be a heavy undertaking, and I think it probable he will require the men on both places to work to advantage. If you & he should think so, you may let him have the Belgrade force to assist him. I leave it, however, to be decided by yourselves. After the work has been commenced you will be better able to decide as to what would be the better course to adopt. Let Aaron examine the machine ropes, in order to determine whether there will be such, and as many as will be required. Should there be more wanting, Henry may purchase them, when he is in Plymouth, from Mr. Willis. Within you will find a note from me to Mr. Willis for that purpose, which he may use if required. If it is not required, he will not use it, but will hand it to me on my return. Henry will not pay for the ropes, if he purchase them, but Mr. Willis will charge them to my account, to be settled when I see him.

Will you examine the lime-house before another letter is sent me from home, and inform me how much lime you think would be required to fill it. Will you inform me whether your Master Charles has shipped a cargo of wheat before your next letter is written, also whether he intends shipping a second cargo when the Lady Whidbee returns, & when she probably will return. I merely ask these questions, perhaps you can answer them readily.

Allen may carry his mother to Mr. Davenport's in a cart. He will then return himself. Affy expressed a wish to carry one of her grandchildren with her; but, after reflection, I am of the opinion it would be best for her not to do so, as the child might be sick, or might give trouble in some way. I hope you have gone on well with harvest & that both corn & wheat are good. Remember me to the people and say to them I hope they are conducting themselves well.

Your friend,
William S. Pettigrew [9]

We are well & leave for the White Sulphur, in Greenbrier County, tomorrow morning. To which place Mr. White will please direct your letters in future.

P.S. Say to Henry, he will require a Fall for removing the stumps from the Creek. It will also be servicable in removing them from the ditch at Belgrade, they being left until a general business may be made of removing them from the ditch. It will be well for him therefore to purchase one from Mr. Willis of Plymouth. The paper enclosed will enable him to do so. Henry will permit Nelson to do some plastering for Dr. Hardison, when the Dr. applies for him. W. S. P.

Sept the 12   1857

My love to master an to master Jonston also. I was glad to receve your letter of the 5 of Sept. on the 12. I began to think thar ware something the matter not hearing no sooner from you. I have commenced fodder on the 8. I got the hands on the 9 of the month. after I get fodder I shall be ready for ditching. it will take about 3 more days in the new ditch. the health of the people is veary good for the season an are conducting themselves well up to this time an all wishes to be remembered to master

Your servant moses an your friend.[10]

October the 10   1857

my love to master. ef master pleases to send 1
1 Brass preserving cittle holding about half bushel
1 cake pan, ef you please. A few cake cutters ef.
1 ice cream freazer an the taile attach to it also if master pleases to do so

Your Servant Polly [11]

Sarah at Magnolia wishes 2 spiders with the tops to them also, ef master pleases.

August the 7, 1858

My love to master an to master Johnston also. Since
we have finished the canals an kept hollydays we have
thrashed the wheat an has got it in order an I tended
to the thrashing of the wheat at Belgrade. I did not
tend to the faning of it. I left it to Dick lake. of the
small Bingham wheat 100 Bushels an of the white
wheat 80 Bushels at Magnolia an I am sorrow that the
wheat did not hold out as well as master. expected. I
thank master I have taken my visit an I saw in plymouth some of master Johnston wheat an expcect
that I have not seen no wheat looks as well as the
Bingham wheat. the white wheat is not as good as it is
in at Belgrade an the rats is so veary bad I would like
for master to send me word what to do with the wheat
at magnolia. if any one wants any seed tha had better
get it away. I could not start the mud mashean while
the thrashing of wheat. the dust was veary bad. I had
no hands to spare for 5 days. the hands will begin on
the mud mashean today. we have not had any rain
since the week you left home an at this time the corn
is suffering veary bad at magnolia all of it. the hands
is all well and doing well. all wishes to be remembered
to master an Polly wishes her love also. I do not wish
to keep any more wheat at magnolia than required
for seed wheat on account of the rats. 18 hats an 18
blankets for men at magnolia. 13 hats an 13 Blankets
for the womens. 9 hats an 9 Blankets for Boys and
girles. 17 childrens Blankets. no hats nor shoes.

Your servant Henry an your friend.[12]

The length an width of the house top at magnolia 20 feet 9 inches the width 22 feet 4 inches the leanth the seames runing the 22 feet 4 inch way. that is the neat measurement. the lowance I leave to master to make himself. shoes for magnolia 1 pare No 12 double soled. 4 pare No 11   3 double soled 1 single soled. 5 pair No 10 double soled. 9 pair No. 9 double soled. 4 pare No 8 double soled. 4 pare No. 7 double soled. 1 pare No. 10 single soled. 2 pare No 9 single soled. 2 pare No 8 single soled. 1 pare No. 7 single soled. 2 pare No 6 single soled. 3 pare No 5 single soled. 1 pare No 4 single soled. 1 pare No 3 single soled.

Shoes for Belgrade

1 pare No 12 double soled. 6 pare No 11 double soled. 3 pare No 10 double soled. 5 pare No 9 double soled. 5 pare No 8 double soled. 2 pare No 7 double soled. 1 pare No 9 single soled. 1 pare No 8 single soled. I pare No 7 single soled. 1 pare No 6 single soled. 2 pare No 5 single soled. all the shoes are taken down. the Boots master can make alowance for them Moses No 12 henry No 10

Despite the use of black drivers, slave discipline at Pettigrew's plantations occasionally broke down during Moses' and Henry's twelve-year reign. In 1850, "two or three unprincipled fellows" led by Frank Buck, a twenty-nine-year-old slave carpenter ("remarkable," as Pettigrew wrote, "for smartness both of body and mind, and no less worthy of note for his lamentable deficiency in common honesty,") cut a trapdoor under the lard-and-meat house at Belgrade, and for some months carried on "a robbery" until he was caught, lodged in irons, forced to confess, and released on the condition that he would become "a better man."

But in the fall of 1857, shortly after Pettigrew had returned from vacation, Frank Buck, apparently in league with Venus, Jack, Patience, and Bill—all field hands—made a duplicate set of keys, robbed the master of $160 in gold and silver, and ran away. As he absconded, Frank Buck (who was, according to Pettigrew, "very polite in his manners when an end is to be gained") informed several white persons whom he encountered on the roads that he had been sent by his master to search for a fugitive. Despite such "art and cunning"—to use Pettigrew's phrase—Frank and his accomplices soon were caught, flogged, and incarcerated. As further punishment, all of the troublemakers were deprived of their ration of molasses; but as late as January 1858, Frank was still refusing to return the stolen money.

Reacting to the slave misconduct, Pettigrew admitted that his confidence was "much impaired," and that he was "apprehensive" about further trouble. As a result, he instituted several repressive measures: he canceled Christmas vacations, on the grounds that the slaves should be "ashamed to be seen away from home after the plantation has been so disgraced by those criminals," and he insisted that Moses and Henry keep him better informed about their business affairs. Pettigrew was, despite continued absence, "more so than ever anxious" and "interested" in them.

Moses & Henry:

As I am yet quietly here, I will write you again, notwithstanding the fact of my having written you several times already. My writing will show the interest I take in my plantations notwithstanding my absence. You perceive my letters are written to both Moses & Henry. This is because I wish to hear from both of you every week. Write particularly about your business as I am anxious about it—more so than I have ever been at any previous absence. The misconduct of some of the people, whilst I was with you, has much impaired my confidence & renders me apprehensive of a renewal of misconduct in some shape or other. Should there be any outbreak requiring my attention, be assured I will be with you within a few days after you have informed me of the fact, in order to adopt such course as circumstances may require.

No molasses is to be given to any one who is confined in the penitentiary; that is, to Frank, Jack or Patience—Nor is Venus to have molasses given her unless she requires it in consequence of sickness. She is not in the penitentiary, I am aware, in consequence of her condition. Do not allow Patience's children to be neglected while she is in the penitentiary. Does Frank make any further confessions as to the money stolen? I have no idea Patience has much of it. During my absence, it is my wish that the people go from home as little as possible. If I were they, I would be ashamed to be seen away from home after the plantation has been so disgraced by those criminals, Jack, Venus, Frank, Patience & Bill. It is painful to me, even now & at this distance from home, to think of such wicked creatures & such crimes. I do not give a positive order, but I think that people had better stay at home during Christmas holidays; no good can result from their going to the Lake, & it might be that some evil would. If no more, it might bring about a quarrel among my people & some of those at the Lake respecting the money stolen by Frank. I wish yourselves & the people at Dr. Hardison's & Mr. Murphy's to keep apart. This, I fear, has not been done, heretofore, as I would wish; and as long as there is a mingling-up of people on different places there must ever be trouble. My idea is, Stay at home & mind your business & let other people mind theirs. . . .

Mr. Johnston & myself are well, and will leave for Charleston after Christmas, where I hope to find letters from home. Yours etc. William S. Pettigrew [13]

$100. Reward.

Runaway from the subscribed on the night of the 6th Nov. negro man, Frank. He is about 5 ft. 9 inches in height, 37 years of age, weighing about 140, of a *dark mulatto* color, not fleshy, some of his teeth rotten in front, with a small scar on his forehead, over one eye, caused by a kick from a horse when a child, and very polite in his manners when an end is to be gained. He is a carpenter. I am informed he has in several instances, since making his escape from my plantation, informed persons whom he has met on the road that he, himself, had been sent by me in search of a runaway. This is mentioned that persons may be on their guard against his art & cunning. Previously to having made his escape, he, by means of false keys, robbed my house of $160. in gold & silver—most of which was of gold.

Any one delivering said man to me, or depositing him in jail, or elsewhere, so that I can obtain possession of him shall have the above reward.

William S. Pettigrew [14]

Scuppernong, Washington Co. N.C.
Nov. 13, 1857

Problems of plantation discipline did not end with the capture of Frank Buck. In 1855, Venus, a field hand, was caught carousing with a friend by the patrol one night.

Bonarva 7 of January, 1855

Mr. William S. Pettigrew
Dear Sir

I take my pen in hand to let you now that I was out paterroleing last night and ketch your venus at 2 oclock. Terry went with her but he doge me. you requsted that I shold let you know if any your peple shold come hear without a pass. tha have been coming without a pass for some time now. I dont now whether you have attend your law or not

most Respecfully yours
S. S. Woodley [15]

One night two weeks later, Dick Bucks was caught with some stolen flour and was turned over to the patrol.

Oct the 9 1858

my love to master an to master Johnston also

I have begun breaking up ground for wheat an the small people picking of peas an have got 100 20 Bishels peas picked. the extra hands are cleaning out the ditches on the s.s. rimmons place have got the main ditch on the road done as has commenced in the 3 feet ditch. master Desired to break up the ground an harrow it an then plow it in with the small plow but the ground is so grassy an rough that it is A thing impossible to be done for the large plow can barely hide the vines an grass an the small plows just leaves the grass all on the top of the ground. in the place whare the hogs is I think we can try it 15 acres. Dick Buck was on Saturday night on the road by Mr Amons Spruels an tha cout him an whiped him an brought him in an said that he had about a gallon of flower. he said first that Mr. lindys man gave it to him an then said that Mr Spruels man gave it to him so the paterolars said an I have whiped him an put him in the penatenrinary of nights an I shall do so until master comes home. the others are all doing veary well up to this time an are only in tolerable health. lizzy is not well. I think that she is got the Bilours some. the old ones wishes thare love to master. Mr. phelps has ben in an altered the hogs on the 5 oct.

your Servant Moses an your friend [16]

Other disputes occasionally broke out on the plantation. Sometimes Moses felt he had to resort to force.

Sept the 25 1858

my love to master an to master Jonston also. I have finished getting fodder. I have not saved as much fodder as I want but it was beat so badly that I got what I could without looseing to much time. I stated to you before that I did not think there would be more corn raised on magnolia than was shiped last an I will say now that I think 3 barrels to the acre is about the yeld. it is the sorrys crop that I ever saw on the place. the creek is up by Mr. Batemans. Aron has finished the Shelter to day. the health of the people is as good as I can expect except Jacob. he is porly today. I have been in the potator patch an looked over them scratched in them. I dont think that tha are veary good. the fracus that I sent the word to master was between me an cousin Jerry. I rang the Bell an Jerry was whiping of the Boy an I told him to stop an he did not an gave words an I hit him an it all was between me an him. as to the work tha have ben faithful. ef more is done I will let master no it. tha are doing veary well now. I was glad to receve masters letter for it has done much good alredy. Polly wishes her love to master [17]

Moses and Henry shared the reins of power with remarkable amicability, perhaps because they were on separate plantations. However, occasionally differences flared.

January the 30, 1858

my love to master an to master Johnston also

the people on Belgrade are all in veary good health an are conducting themselves veary well up to this date. tha all wish to be remembered to master. henry come to me after Brandy an you now Master that Brandy is A veary particular thing. I did not let him have it. you did not tell me to do so an ef you wish him to have any you will pleas answer the question. master I do not think that you told me anything about it before leaving home. one week 2½ days since I comenced after being hendered other ways. 12 fellars 83 post up to this time.

> Your servant Moses an your friend [18]
your servant Aron

Despite its problems, Pettigrew apparently never seriously considered abandoning his system of black overseers. When Moses died, Pettigrew elevated Glasgow, Moses' cousin, to the post of overseer, indicating his determination to continue using drivers for accommodationist purposes. "Glasgow possesses many qualities that will, I think if cultivated, adapt him to his present position," Pettigrew wrote. "He is honest, industrious, not too *talkative* (which is a necessary qualification), a man of good sense, a good hand himself, and has been heretofore faithful in the discharge of whatever may have been committed to his care. He is but thirty two years of age [which] may militate against him [only] for a short while . . . [for] withal, the young man grows up with the business of the plantation, and it becomes *incorporated in his very mind* [italics added]."

My dear Sister,

> Please accept my thanks for your very kind and affectionate letter of the 21st ult., in which you make especial allusion to the death of my faithful Servant, Moses. He is entitled to all that any one can say in his praise; and, as to my own feelings, I shall ever regard it a duty and a pleasure to cherish for his memory the highest respect, as long as I retain any recollection of the merits of those who have aided me in acting my part amid the toils of life. I humbly trust he has exchanged the duties of this world for the rest & enjoyment of a better. If so, the loss is only ours, the

gain is his. In the management of the plantation, Glasgow is his substitute; who is a cousin of poor Moses and a son of old uncle Bill—the latter of whom was my foreman at the time of his death in 1844. Glasgow possesses many qualities that will, I think if cultivated, adapt him to his present position. He is honest, industrious, not too *talkative* (which is a necessary qualification) a man of good sense, a good hand himself, and has been heretofore faithful in the discharge of whatever may have been committed to his care. He is but thirty two years of age. His comparative youth may militate against him for a short while—but only for a short while, if he prove to be in possession of the abilities requisite for his station. The man of 32 will, in ten years' time, find in any company of persons a far greater number behind him than are in advance of him. It will be many years before those disqualifications for command that usually characterize old persons will overtake the man of 30; While he who has attained 50 must soon expect the inexorable hand of time to soften that vigour which is all important in a ruler and without which he soon permits some stronger spirit than his own to assume the mastery over him. Withal, the young man grows up with the business of the plantation, and it becomes incorporated in his very mind. Dick Lake is a faithful man, & I have no doubt would have administered the affairs of the place well. . . .

Believe me, my dear Sister, your affectionate brother,

W. S. Pettigrew [19]

Black overseers managed the plantations and mills of many other prominent Southerners, among them Judge Charles Tait and his son, James Asbury Tait, who moved from Georgia to Wilcox County, Alabama, between 1817 and 1819. Farming cotton and corn on a small scale at first, the Taits by 1835 had increased their holdings to about 180 slaves and several thousand acres of rich land. In the summer of 1826 the Taits dismissed two white overseers "for unoverseerlike conduct in permitting the negroes to become disorderly and 'rebellious' . . . and for making 2 of the men run away by threatening to shoot them for a trifling cause." A slave named Harford was therefore elevated to the position of overseer. Soon afterward, Harford dictated a letter to his master. Harford continued to serve the Tait family in various positions of responsibility at least until 1842.

Mobile Nov. 6th 1826

My Dear Master

Your kind favor to me through Mr Claiborne has been duly recd. and I now hasten to answer the same and inform you how your affairs are going here. I left the plantation the 31st. Ultimo, at which time they were coming on very well with the crop. Eighty Bales had then been packed, and they think they will have Eighty more. I think the cotton is much cleaner than it was last year. The corn crop is very good, and I think they will have plenty for the next year. I saw Master James the Day I left, who told me his Family was well, and that he would soon send them to the plantation to stay a few weeks, and I am sorry to have to inform you that nine of the children have died at the Plantation, mostly with the Hooping Cough, and the old woman Peggy has been very low for the last three months,—when on the way down to this place I stoped at [torn] Claiborne and cleaned out the garden and put everything in the same order as when you left, and [————?] has been very attentive to the House, and has had every thing Suned, frequently—I have been generally well this summer except two short attacs of fever. Sylvia has been very ill, for some time, but she is now recovering, and I hope she will soon be well. Sarah has been well during the summer, and Nancy is now well, after a little indisposition. There will be five Births at the plantation and among the Number, Nancy is to give birth to one, after a suspension of fourteen years—Mr. Wade is to leave soon for Georgia, from whence he will return in december. he requested me to know of Mrs. whether she would be willing for Sarah to come to Mobile, and stay During the winter. She has stayed at Mr. Walkers during the summer at 8 Dollars per month, which is all she can get there. She is therefore anctious to come to Mobile where she can make 12 Dollars per month. I have seen Mr. Black, the waggon maker, who says he will have the waggon finished the last of this month. Times have been so hard that I have made but little for myself as yet, but I am in hopes that I shall now do better. All those at the plantation wish to be remembered to you and Mrs. as well as those at Claiborne. Also your most obt svt. and my little family who are very well. And I have an little son named after myself—[torn] I hopes ever to merit your esteem—

Your Most dutiful Servant

Harford [20]

[37]

In the 1840's, Simon Gray, a slave, was hired by the Andrew Brown Lumber Company of Natchez to supervise the rafting of lumber and sand the company sent down the Mississippi River. Gray directed as many as twenty raftsmen, both slaves and whites. He disciplined the crewmen, dispersed wages of about $20 monthly to the white workers and overtime payments to the slaves, and paid the expenses of both. After each trip, Gray returned to Natchez by steamboat with his crew.

Gray was an exceptionally capable manager. Guiding hundred-foot rafts down the twisting rivers required great skills, and bargaining with planters and sawmillers demanded considerable business sense. Gray, who knew how to read, write, and keep accurate accounts, collected and disbursed large sums of money. Once he delivered $800 to a creditor and on another occasion he escorted a newly purchased bondsman from the slave market to an industrial site, fulfilling responsibilities ordinarily entrusted only to white men. He lived with his family in a rented house, charged goods to his personal account at the company store, and was allowed vacations at Hot Springs, Arkansas. Still, Gray also reduced the management costs of the lumber company. As a head raftsman Gray at first received $12 monthly, or about one-quarter of the wages of a white head raftsman. Even when his incentive pay was raised to $20 per month, the same wages as an ordinary white raftsman, it was but half that of a white supervisor.

Although Gray was one of the most privileged of all Southern slaves, his vision of freedom nevertheless exceeded his exceptional status. Once he bilked the lumber company by rafting logs for his personal profit; sometimes he purposely missed the earliest boat back to Natchez to gain more time on his own in New Orleans. In July 1863, Gray's name vanished without explanation from the company's rolls, indicating that he had fled to Union lines (along with Jim Mathews, whose responsibilities and privileges almost equaled Gray's) during the battle of Vicksburg.

Gray usually kept his own records, but occasionally a bookkeeper helped him when the work became burdensome. On long trips Gray usually submitted reports to his employers. Although Gray had been taught to read and write in 1847, some of his letters, reports, and accounts may have been dictated.

Plaquemine, June 21st 1850

Andrew Dott
Sir

I now write you these few lines to let you know that I am a little better than I was when I left. I have got along quite well with the boate so far and have delivered *Mr. Moss* bill according to order and takena draft for the same. I stopped the boat from leaking in the evening of the 19th of this month. This bill of Mr. Allens, it is to come with H. K. Moss next bill. I have not made any collections as yet but have the promis of some this morning. This letter that I send in your care I want to send to my wife, if you please.

Nothing more at preasant. I remain your umble servant &c.

Simon Gray [21]

Yazoo City   Januy 25 1857

Andrew Brown Esqr
Natchez
Sir

I have closed the trade for the Lumber at $16 pr M   There is about 3000 feet 1 Inch plank   the balance 1¼ 1½ &2 inch   I was just in time to get it   Mr

SIMON GRAY'S ACCOUNT OF HIS SAND TRIPS TO N. ORLEANS

By Receipts of trip in March

By amt. from Mrs. Vaughn	$	20	00	
" " " Winchester		20	00	
" " from Lepiere for Boat & 800 bbls		400	00	
		$ 440	00	

To Expenses of trip

For Boat—	130	00			
" Provisions &c	14	50			
" Men—	29	50			
" Boys Scott &c	20	25			
" Passages—	20	00	214	25	
By balance made on trip			$ 225	75	

By Receipts of trip in April

By amt for 250 bbls	$	100	00		
" " " 20 "		8	00		
" " " 20 "		8	00		
" " " 120 "		48	00		
" " " 15 "		6	00		
" " " 150 "		52	50		
" Amt for Boat &c		100	00	322	50

To Expenses of the trip

for men &c	$	77	50		
" amt for Boat		80	00		
" passages & men		20	20	177	70
			$ 144	80	

By Receipts of trip in May & June

By Case from J. H. Riggin on a/c		$ 80	00
" Sale of Flat Boat		65	00
" Bal from Riggin		765	70
		$ 910	70

To Expenses for the trip as per a/c

" rend'd by Mr. Key	317	90		
" lumber for flooring Boat	33	00		
" amt for Boat	100	00	450	90
			$ 459	80

By Receipts of Clay Boat.

By amt for sand to Brisden	116	00		
" " for Flat Boat	25	00		
" " " Clay to Bennet	237	15	378	15

To Expenses of trip as per a/c

rend'd by Mr. Key	182	25			
" Towage on Clay Boat	15	00			
" Provisions on trip down	7	00			
" Wharfage	10	00	$ 241	25	
			163	00	

Sand Boat		459	80
		$ 623	70
To Amt of A. L. Wilson's bill		83	57
		$ 540	13
To Cost of Clay Boat		50	00
		$ 490	13

SOURCE: From the Andrew Brown Miscellaneous Financial Papers, 1856, Learned Collection, Lumber Archives, University of Mississippi Archives, Oxford.

Klein had sent a man up and he arrived there in one hour after I had closed the bargain he offered $18 for the lot. I have thought it best to go to Greenwood and see about the boat and drop it down and then will either come or send to you for hands nothing more but remain yours

Simon Gray [22]

Slave managers and drivers were also used by the Reverend Charles Colcock Jones of Georgia to assist in the operation of his plantations. Jones was the eloquent pastor of Savannah's First Presbyterian Church who became the leading proponent of formal religious training for slaves. Indeed, as early as 1831 he had delivered a sermon urging Southerners to instruct their slaves in Christian principles in order to create "a greater subordination" among them and to teach "respect and obedience [to] all those whom God in His providence has placed in authority over them." The minister seemed concerned for the salvation of slaves' souls, but he stressed that religion should be consciously used to discipline and control the slave population—that is, as he said, to support "the peace, the order, the purity, the happiness, and the prosperity of our Southern country." Moreover, Jones firmly believed that "a faithful servant is more profitable than an unfaithful one," and both his widely used "slave catechism" and his famous pamphlet *Suggestions on the Religious Instruction of the Negroes in the Southern States* [23] were being reprinted as late as 1862.

The Reverend Jones had an opportunity to practice what he preached, for after 1832 he operated three rice plantations in Liberty County, Georgia. Jones was often absent from his estates, spreading his gospel around the South, teaching "ecclesiastical history" at a Columbia, South Carolina, theological seminary, and spending several months each year in Philadelphia at the offices of the Presbyterian Board of Domestic Missions. To manage the plantations in his absence, Jones employed at least two white overseers (John S. Stevens and Thomas J. Shepard), to whom he sent letters of instructions. Under these whites worked three black managers: Cato, the foreman at Montevideo, Andrew, the driver at Maybank, and Sandy Maybank, the head carpenter. With these three slaves, as well as with others, Jones carried on an unusual correspondence.

Jones attempted to accommodate his work force to bondage mainly through careful instruction in Christian beliefs, and was hopeful that his slave managers would transmit conservative religious ideas to the field hands. "I trust you are holding on in your high profession of the Gospel of our Lord and Saviour Jesus Christ at all times, and constantly watch and pray," Jones wrote to Sandy, after directing the slave to complete some work. "I hope God will be with you and give you good health again," the master advised Cato, expressing similar sentiments. "You know our life and health are in His hands, and it is a great comfort to me to have a good hope that you love Him, and do put all your trust in our Lord and Saviour Jesus Christ, who" concluded Jones, "is a precious Saviour to us in life and death." By thus urging his slaves to place their faith in religious salvation, Jones attempted to promote plantation discipline.

Philad. Jan 28, 1851

Dear Cato,

I got Mr. Shepard's good letter this morning, in which he gives me a very particular account of all your work and business on the Plantation, and it all pleases me well. You have got along finely, and when Mr. Rahn & Majr. Porter pay you up what they owe you, you will pretty well close up the marsh, which will be a great improvement to the place, and be a light to all who see it.

But I am very sorry—& very much troubled to hear how sick you have been: and feel grateful to Mr. Shepard for his prompt attention to you. Now you must take every necessary care of yourself. Have you a plenty of flannel? I wish you to get Mr. Shepard to get you some good flannel & have your *shirts made of it, coming down well over the hips, with long sleeves & two or three pair of Drawers of the same:* & so keep yourself warmly clad. Let Phoebe cut them out & make them at once & nicely for you, and whatever *outer* clothing you want, Mr. Shepard will get for you.

You must pay attention to what you eat: Have your victuals cooked regularly and carefully. Make what arrangements you think best for this. Eat at the same times every day and do not exercise in the dew or wet. Carry your cloak & umbrella, and have you good fires—and be sure to sleep warm. If you fancy anything special to eat, Mr. Shepard will see that you have it. Keep your feet dry with thick heavy shoes or Boots. I hope God will be with you & give you good health again. You know our life and health are in His hands, and it is a great comfort to me to have a good hope that you love Him, and do put all your trust in our Lord and Saviour Jesus Christ, who is a precious Saviour to us in life and in death. We have been together a long time, and I have always had a great attachment to you and confidence in you: and you have always been a good and faithful man to me. And now that we are apart from one another, & you are sick it makes me feel a great deal. But I hope you will soon be up again. Be careful of the cold, damp & changeable weather in February or March. Mr. Shepard will

point out some one of the men, who can take a look
after things when you are not able to be as much
about as you wish, and he can take directions from
you and make his report to you.

Am glad to hear the small-pox is pretty much
over, and that the people have all behaved well, and
kept away from it. This pleases me much. It is great
mercy in the Lord that He did not suffer it to spread:
for it is a dreadful disease, and many would no doubt
have died of it; and many too, who would not have
been prepared to die. We ought to think much of the
Lord's mercies to us, who are unworthy of every one
of them. I long to come home and see all the people at
Monte-Video and Arcadia, & at the Island: and see
how they do, and how you are all getting along.
There is not a day that I do not think of you—and
daily as I bow my knees before God, I try to remember you in my prayers, that He would be mer-
ciful to you and bless you all.—Tell all the people
howdye for me, *name by name*—from Tony and Flora
& Rosetta down: and your Mistress and Miss Mary &
Master Charles & Joe, send Howdye for all too. We
have all been pretty well up to this time. Yesterday
your Miss Mary was taken with fever & chill from a
bad cold, and it kept on all night, until this morning.
The Doctor came to see her, & she is much better &
we hope will have no more of it. We have quit the
Boarding House we first went to and have gone to
another which we like better. We do not like boarding
as well as living in our own House, but we cannot afford to go to Housekeeping now. It would cost too
much, and besides we dont know the ways of the

country well enough yet. They have white servants and black servants: some good & some bad. Some of the black people do pretty well, but a great many of them are badly off—and about as bad as they well can be.—We have had it a great deal colder here than at home, and the cold has been very good for me. It has braced me up & made me feel better, & I have wished for it to be colder. Now it is very mild. Charles & Joe were with us some four weeks & better: both very well—and doing very well at their Books. Their Teachers speak highly of them. They are very sober, good young men & we have much comfort in them. They have not professed religion yet. We can't be at peace until we have good hope through grace, that they are good Christians. They went back to College last Thursday. We heard from them on Saturday. The small-pox is in Princeton where they are: but altogether among the *black people.* Hope they may not have it.—We have no special life in religion in this great City. The Churches seem to get along only tolerably well. There are a great many things here to make people forget God. I am kept very busy: & preach somewhere most every Sabbath. Preached for the Black-people a few Sabbaths ago. But it was a bad afternoon, and but a poor turn out. They do not do very well in religion. I send you *something* in this letter for yourself: a little *New-Years present.* Tell Mr. Shepard, I will write him soon: & that his letter was all good. You must send me a letter & let me know how you are. Very truly yours—*C. C. Jones.* [24]

Cato and Andrew inform their master of events on the plantation.

Montie Viedieo   Septr 3ᵈ 1852

Dear Master—Mr Shepard brought me your letter
last week, and I heard it read to me with great pleasure, and much obliged to you Master for your kind
notice of me. I always feel satisfied that I have a good
Shear of your Love and Confidance, but whenever I
See you take the time & trouble, to write me your Servant a kind & and I may say fatherly letter, it makes
me feel more like crying with love & grattitude for So
kind a master than any thing else, and always feel it in
my heart to say, I will try and be a better Servant than
ever   Be sure it is a great Satisfaction & pleasure to
me, and I believe I can safely say to all my fellow servants to hear that our young Masters are doing well,
and that they dont let none [of] the other young people go before them, for niggar as I am, I want my
child to behave better and be Smarter or as Smart as
anybodys children, and besides I know without any
boddys telling me, how it would greeve my Dear Master and Mistress if my young masters did not come
up to their expectation. I always thought Mass Chaley
was like his pa & if he lived would make a Smart man,
but I dont understand, why he is going to learn Lawyer, we all thought when he got his larning he would
be a preacher, But Sandy Maybank say taint to late
yet. look at Mr. Stiles he learn Lawyer first and is now
one of the biggest preachers, as whats wanting, we
every one of us is well pleased to hear about our
young Masters & Missie

Mʳ Law preached last Sunday at Cross roads and
I had an oportunity of seeing most of the Watchmen

and Drivers you mentioned & all. All, Everyone was more than glad to hear from you & all send Tousend howdys for you. Toney Stevens says he is going to write you a letter—Your people all seem to be doing very well. They attend praise & go to church regularly whenever there is preaching in reach. We have had a good deel of Sickness among the children from worms, but no verry ill cases. Sinas youngest child Frank was taken last week with a breaking out on all its Thighs & Bottom & privates   The Skin appeared to be thick & blackish. Something like a burn Mr Shepard thot at first it was. and again from its privates being So much Swolen thought it was a bad disorder but satisfying himself that big Adam & Sina both were clean of such a thing he could not tell what it could be, but tryed first one thing and then another intending if he Saw no change for the better to call a Doctor, but before he did So the Child died, the bowels was kept gently open with oil, and the erruption was anointed with a healing salve & finding it looked So badly Mr Shepard had an application of honey & Suth to dry it up & he is somewhat of the opinion he may have done wrong in drying it up too suddenly—All are now well excepting Phoeboe & her whole family. They are up & down some one everyday with fevers. I have gottin away all the worms from Lafayette Lizzie & Victoria & Mr Shepard says we must not grieve them any more medicine, but try & break the fevers with Thumowroot tea, & dogwood & cherry bark. None of them are ever verry sick but cant get clear of the fever. Old Clarisa is also quite unwell.

We are this week working on the roads with our men. I have been for parts of two weeks on our marsh

Stopping the big cut which I am Satisfied is now Secure & Raising the river dam all round which is a big job & will take up much time yet but you will be pleased with the way we are putting it up. We wont have any time to cut any new ground this year, Mr. Shepard says he has receved your last letter & you advise that a finis should be made to all the back work & the fences properly made & we are glad that is your mind & think So too. The Carpenters wont be done fixing for the bricks till next week & then Mr S Says he will go right to it he says he aught to have commenced the 1st Sept but wont Start till all things are in propper fixture, The heavy rains in August & hot Sun has damaged us in the cotton much   All the unmannured ground is more or less blighted & in Spots looks like winter but the manured ground though diseased holds on well. The marsh has astonished Every boddy that has seen it   it is very fine cotton & Especially all the oldest Stocks from the first planting, we have now all the women picking cotton & from appearance will have no more time to do anything else   it is opening finely & is very white & pretty cotton   I think we will make Thirty Bales unless I am much dicieved The cattepillers are all over the county & as near us as Maj Porters, but not in ours yet & the people Say So far they are not doing much damage. The rice crop Looks fair all things considered, & we cant Say yet much about it   it is new ground rice never regular, but in bunches & Spots & always looks better Standing than when all hauled together, but I am in hopes will come up to last year. We will break in corn week after next, we have made a fine crop of corn from all appeerence & from the great Quantity of foder we have Saved. Our Hop Crop is nothing like as

[49]

good as we usually have. The reason is the vines was rather young when the Season Set in & after we planted they were set & out of danger the heavy rains & hot Scorching Sun Scaulded them. The pease Crop is not as good as we Expected but fair & perhaps will make as much as we will find time to pick. I got 5 Allowances from Maybanks, & one from Arcadia which was all Mr Rhan Says he could spair. Mr Shepard Says he can Loan us Two allowances from Major Porters which will do us till we harvest—I am trying to make all the manure I can for I See more & more the good of it. I have now told you all I can think of & hope Dear Master you & Missus & my young Master & Miss Mary may keep well & that the Lord will be with you all & that we may live to Sea Each other again Negar Philly & Rose particularly Says put our names in the Letter to tell Master & Mistress howdy & all the rest sends howdy

Your Servant *Catoe* [25]

Mr Shepard Sends howdy too, & Says it will be his turn to wright next which he will do week after next after he has finished breaking in the Corn So as to Let you know how much. All this time Corn was Scarce Lightfoot & Jacksen had to take a plenty of fodder but Eat Corn on promise but now as Soon as we harvest they shall have it

Catoe

Maybank
10th Septr 1852

My dear Master,

When Mas John [Stevens, the overseer,] read
your letter to me I was in the garden with the rest of
the people choping it out and preparing to plant
pease, which I have since done; he called us all
around him so that we could hear every word, and
really master you dont know how good we felt to hear
that you and Mistress and my young Masters & Mis-
seys are all well and living in your own hired house;
and that Mas Charles come out so well, and was guine
to be a Philadelphia lawyer, I have always heard that
they can out talk all the other sort of lawyers, I only
hope that after he practices his profession for a short
time he may put it aside like the blessed St Paul and
take to preaching the gospel. I have had your letter in
my pockets ever since, and we all agreed that it was
the most *affectionate* and *beautiful* letter we ever heard
read. . . . I almost forgot to tell you that you liked
never to have seen Old Andrew and most of us in this
world again, for in June last when we were working in
the cotton field among the old live oaks during a
thunder storm, a flash of lightning struck one of the
old oaks and shivered it to attomes throwing limbs as
large as my body full a task from the main tree. We
were not more than two tasks off at the time and saw
the *fire* and smelt the brimstone, but thanks to a kind
Providence we all escaped unharmed but with this
reflection brought more vividly before us that in the
"midst of life we are in death"—About a month ago
Rev^d Mr Law administered tha sacraments in Sunbury

and among several black people that joined the church was my daughter Dinah, and I trust that she may practice what she professes, for as Mas John says it is no light thing to be a christian, for we may play with the lightning and the rattle snake, but dont trifle with Almighty God "least he tear you to pieces in his anger and then be never to deliver you"—Now my dear Master I believe I have told you all, and after sending love to you all from myself and all the people, I remain as I trust I may always be Your faithful servant

Andrew [26]

Although Jones's arrangements seemed effective, especially with privileged slaves, discipline was never complete; even religious instruction could not guarantee that there would not be backsliders and recalcitrants. In this regard, the slave correspondence is especially revealing of the lives of two bondsmen, named Phoebe and Cash, who were "married." Cash was, according to the records, a field hand, while Phoebe served as a seamstress and sometimes worked in the fields. Phoebe and Cash were apparently a very troublesome couple; indeed, in 1851, Cato reported to Jones on the problems of managing these two blacks. Ever since Cash has been living with Phoebe, complained Cato, "I am afraid he has given himself up to the old boy . . . [and] he appears more petulent and has not only given up going to prayers but I have several times heard him make use of bad words whenever he was displeased." Using religion as a means of control, Cato brought Cash's case before the local minister, who in turn "cited" him in front of the next church service. "Phoebe and I get along So, So," reported the driver. "So far as yet, She does her work very well, but there is [she has] a strong notion now and then to break out, but she knows well Enough how it will be if She does, and I am in hope she will let her better judgment rule her passions."

Monday Evening Monteviedieo 3 Mar 1851

Dear Master

I received your kind letter, and when Mr Shepard was reading it to me on the Marsh Dam, I felt Thankful to god for So good a master and it made me feel Melancholy to think you & Mistress who I knew loved & felt for me was so far away, and the uncertainties of our lives. May be we Shall never again look on one another, but be this as it may, we know one thing if we live as we aught death cant Separate us, though it may do so for a little while.

I had been verry sick but was much better and up, when I got your letter, but quite feble and from that time to this I have not laid up any more but still I have not mended as I was in hopes to have done. I was taken with a bad cold and a year ache & teeth ache and all together made me feel verry bad but now I am mending Slowly. I try and take all the care of myself I can, and Mr Shepard scolds me all the while, and you way younder is cautioning me makes me think sometimes I am Really worse off than I think I am, My Cloathing is all good and warm, and If I nead anything at all I will apply to Mr Shepard as you direct me to do. And Send you my great Thanks for the kindness & love which I know you have for me and also for the Newyears present your letter contained which was handed me by Mr Shepard for which I thank you much, but besides all this, I feel thankful Master, for Your Memorance of me, when you bow befor god, And beg you Still to do so for his and your poor unwordy Servant, and I will do so for

[53]

you the best I can. I wish to live right, and Serve god faithfully, & be prepared, let death come Sooner or Later, and I know I cant be unfaithful to my Earthly Master, and faithful to god. but I feel it in me If I am faithful to my heavenly Master the best I Can, then Every Thing Else goes right. We have had some Sickness Since Mr Shepard last wrote you Fanny was threatened with Pleurisy for several days but is up and well again. And Negar was taken verry violently on Saturday week last. I gave oil & Blistered and poulticed and he grew So Much worse as though the pain in his Side would Cut away his breath that I could not risque to wait till day light but Sent John off to Mr. Shepard who soon as he got the word Sent Dr King who came a little before day and found him badly off and after taking a heap of blood & Enlarging the blister, gave relief Mr Shepard kept him in the house all this week and would not suffer him to come out fearing a relapse until this morning, he is now out again. Negar has been living very Carelessly and Indiferent to his duty as a Christian would not attend prayers, but this Sudden Sickness Seems to have made him think better I have talked to him and I hope hereafter he has made up his mind to do better. As for Cash I am afraid he has given up himself to the old boy, for Since his wife has been with him he appears more petulent and has not only given up going to prayers, but I have several times heard him make use of bad words Whenever he was displeased, & have shamed and talked to him so often, that I have felt it my duty to report him to the church & Mr Law has Cited him before the Next Meeting. Phoebe and I get along So, So. So far as yet, She does her work very well, but there is a strong notion now and then to break out but She knows well Enough how it will be if

She does, and I am in hopes she will let her better judgment rule her passions. As for all the Women I have Nothing to Complain of in their religious duties they all Seem willing and are punctual as the hour of Prayer and am in hopes are trying to live Christian lives. Mr Winn has spent one night with us at Monteviedieo preaching and Chatikized the Children, preached once Since at Pleasant Grove, and is to administer the ordinances there next Sabbath. I make all the children go out. We are all much pleased with Mr Winn, and hope he will come as often as he can.

Little Cash & Wally are both sick today with urasipalis. I gave Each a dose of Saltse before Mr Shepard came & he has just sent to the Boro for a little Sulphur to give in this morning in milk & afterwards the Elder tea. All the rest of the people are well, and all Send howdy to you and Misstress and Miss Miss Mary & Mass Charles and Mass Josey. Mariah belonging to Mass Joseph Anderson (Driver Georges Wife) died last week. . . .

Tony Stevens tells me he has recd a letter from you & is well pleased & is to meet Mr Shepard here some night & will wright you. We are all glad to hear of you Speaking of paying us a visit this Spring. *I hope* my Dear Master god will be with you and our Dear Mistress & all your Children and that they may always do well. Mr Shepard sends howdy to you all with me. he has been quite unwell with soar throat, but is better

Your dutiful Servant
Catoe Jones [27]

(Mr Shepard will write
you next week)

[55]

Over the next six years, Cash's cussing and Phoebe's passions became so unruly that Cato could not control them. So, despite his religious principles, which once led him to admire certain plans of manumission and colonization, Jones decided to dispose of these two slaves along with several members of their family. They were placed with a slave-trader and shipped to New Orleans for sale. From there they apparently found an opportunity to write back to their family and friends on the old plantation. Since their letter was written even *before* they had been sold to a new master, it is one of the few remaining direct expressions by blacks caught up in the interstate slave traffic.

Phoebe and Cash's letter demonstrates their complete consciousness of their predicament. "Although we were sold for spite," they proclaimed, "we hope it is for our own good, but we cannot be doing any better than [this]. we are doing very well. . . . Please tell Cato," they continued with open hostility for their former driver and their previous living conditions, "that what [food] we have got to throw away now it would be enough to furnish your Plantation for one season."

Throughout their letter the two slaves never mention either their master or any member of his family, suggesting that they had not assimilated Jones's concept of a family of coreligionists. On the other hand, Phoebe and Cash do send messages to many members of their *own* family, indicating that while they had refused to absorb Jones's paternalism they had been able to retain their own family ties. Moreover, Phoebe and Cash's letter is entirely nonreligious in tone. This secularism pertains even when the slaves send their love to old friends and their immediate family—a point at which other slave [and nonslave] letters usually break into religious language. The secular character of the letter suggests again that Phoebe and Cash never assimilated Jones's religious instructions; they kept their independence to the end.

New Orleans March 17th 1857

Mr Delions

Pleas tell my daugher Clairissa and Nancy a heap how a doo for me Pheaby and Cash and Cashes son James we left Savanah the first of Jany we are now in New Orleans. Please tell them that their sister Jane died the first of Feby we did not know what was the matter with her some of the doctors said that she had the Plurisly and some thought that she had the Consumption. although we were sold for spite I hope that it is for our own good but we cannot be doing any better than we are doing very well. Mr Delions will please tell Cato that what [food] we have got to t[h]row away now it would be anough to furnish your Plantation for one season Mr Delions will please answer this Letter for Clairssa and Let me know all that has hapend since i left. Please tell them that the Children were all sick with the measles but they are all well now. Clairssa your affectionate mother and Father sends a heap of Love to you and your Husband and my Grand Children Phebea. Mag. & Cloe. John. Judy. Sue. My aunt Aufy sinena and Minton and Little Plaska. Charles Nega. Fillis and all of their Children. Cash. Prime. Laffatte. Rick Tonia [sends their love] to you all. Give our Love to Cashes Brother Porter and his wife Patience. Victoria gives her Love to her Cousin Beck and Miley

I have no more to say untill i get a home. I remain your affectionate Mother and Father

Pheobia and Cash [28]

[57]

P.S. Please give my love to Judys Husband Plaska and also Cashs love. Pheobe and Cash send a great deal of Howdie for Mr Adam Dunumn and Mr Samuel Braton.

In 1858, Jones sold Abream Scriven, who wrote a poignant letter to his wife Dinah, who had remained on Jones's estate.

Savannah Sept the 19 1858

Dinah Jones

My Dear wife I take the pleasure of writing you these few [lines] with much regret to inform you that I am Sold to a man by the name of Peterson atreader and Stays in new orleans. I am here yet But I expect to go before long but when I get there I will write and let you know where I am. My Dear I want to Send you Some things but I donot know who to Send them By but I will thry to get them to you and my children. Give my love to my father & mother and tell them good Bye for me. and if we Shall not meet in this world I hope to meet in heaven. My Dear wife for you and my Children my pen cannot Express the griffe I feel to be parted from you all

I remain your truly husband until Death
Abream Scriven [29]

Another slave (not, however, one of Jones's) on the brink of being sold pleads for rescue from the horrors of the slave trade.

June th 6 1804

Dear sir   I now tak this oportunity to let you kow that
I am well and Hopeing thes few lines will find you the
same   I am very sory that you think so litle of me   If
it was In my power as it is in yours I wowld Dow more
for yu but I am A Slave and ever expect to be for all
you mean to do for me dear sisters And brothers I am
sory that you Think so litle of me and I hope that if
we dont met here that we will meet here after and i
expect to be sold every moment and If you men to
Dow any thing for me Dow know as soon posible I
heard buy Mr Jackson that Jery migha [Jeremiah]
gipsen was a comming on but he has not come yet
And I am very sory for it   And I should to know the
reason of his not comming for I am here A wayting
with a Greyte deal of pasianc [patience]

I have no more to say at Present

I Remain your affectionate And lovein brother
James Gipson [30]

The mother of all these
Charity matheus
Zila king
Jersey johnson
Caty matheus
Silva matheus
William mathus
This is by Jams gipson
Sent by John John jackson
for to find you all out

And if he dous find you out
If he you this to Remind you that I am in a very bad
way Aand expect to be sold evry day And I learnt Mr
Jackson that Jersy gipson was a coming on I had no
more time at present

James gip son

CHAPTER TWO

House Servants

THE "CAVALIER MYTH" required slaveholders to have a retinue of black servants on their estates to make them appear as self-sufficient, gracious, and hospitable as possible. Wealthy planters therefore frequently used slaves as cooks, waiters, butlers, maids, hostelers, and coachmen at their townhouses and plantation mansions. Of all blacks, these household slaves (who were sometimes the mulatto offspring of the masters themselves) had the least contact with the field hands and the greatest intimacy with the white family. Trained from childhood, house servants were raised to believe that they were superior in status and importance to other bondsmen—a belief reinforced by the better food, clothing, and extra privileges they received. When they might chance to join other bondsmen in revolt the fear of demotion to the field often held them in line. Yet, the extent to which they formed a separate caste is open to debate. Even in the isolation of the "big house," ties of color, blood, and common oppression were never obliterated.

Masters considered domestic servants to be the most accommodating and submissive of all slaves. Some house slaves were encouraged to identify so closely with their master's interests that they tattled on overseers, spied on fellow bondsmen, and revealed insurrectionary plans. Yet precisely because they lived under a special oppression and knew their masters so intimately, house servants could become deceptive, murderous, and rebellious. Domestics were, after all, in an excellent position to "hustle" favors, practice "put-ons," steal goods, poison their owners' food or water, and collaborate with dissatisfied field hands and industrial bondsmen in uprisings or escapes, as occurred in the Denmark Vesey conspiracy.

One Southerner who employed many household slaves was David Campbell, a wealthy Abingdon, Virginia, planter who served as governor from 1837 to 1841. Campbell, a Jacksonian Democrat who deserted the party and became a Whig in 1840, was noted for his early advocacy of a state common school system. While in office, Campbell lived in Richmond with his wife, Mary, and his daughter, Virginia, and he also brought to the governor's mansion some of his house servants, including Michael Valentine, an elderly butler; Eliza Dixon and Richard, Michael's daughter and son; and David, Michael's younger son. Campbell left behind at Montcalm, his valley estate (under the stewardship of a Mr. Latham), his other house servants, including Hannah Valentine, the elderly wife of Michael; Aunt Lucinda (Lucy) and Aunt Lethe Jackson, Hannah's two sisters who worked as cooks and gardeners; and Mary and some of the other children of Eliza Dixon.

Campbell's departure for Richmond and the separation of his slaves resulted in a correspondence among the slaves themselves as well as between the plantation slaves and their owners in the city. Two rare letters from one house servant to another were written, and two letters from house slaves to their mistresses followed. Although these letters were apparently dictated by the blacks to a white scribe, they nonetheless suggest some of the house servants' feelings toward themselves, their families, and their master. Especially striking are the strong feelings expressed for their own black relatives and family, as well as for their master and mistresses. The detailed information about plantation and neighborhood affairs, their own activities, and the behavior of other slaves and of the overseer suggests that the slave community was not bound by plantation lives. Significant, too, are their strong belief in Christianity and their awareness of their own obedience, protection of their master's interests, and dependence on their owners for orders, direction, and approval. But the house servants' apparent acceptance of white domination should not be equated with complete submissiveness, as is indicated by their continual quest for greater privileges.

Hannah Valantine and "Aunt" Lethe Jackson report on life on the old plantation.

Abingdon May 2ᵈ 1838

My dear Mistress

I was very much gratified at receiving a letter from you last monday. When I was writing to Richard I thought you would like to hear particularly about every thing at home and as it gave you pleasure I am very glad that I did mention something about it. We were all very uneasy about you when we heard you were confined to your bed, for we knew that you must be very sick if that was the case. I cannot tell you how much pleased I was to hear that you were well enough to walk about your room, and I shall be still more so when I hear you are riding out for I think that will be of more service to you than any thing else. I hope by this time you are well enough to be preparing for your trip to the north, and I long for the time to come when I shall see you & my dear master & miss Virginia at home once more, not to speak of Michael and my children.

Miss Ellen White received Miss Virginia's letter, and told me she had answered it some time ago. I expect it will not be long before Miss Ellen and Master Thomas will be in Richmond. I heard that they will set off on Tuesday next. Mr Humes set off to the

North yesterday. I heard that Miss Mitchel & Melville were at Col. Whites, and went down to see them, but they had gone to Mr. Clapp's. Miss Ellen White told me all that they said about you all, how you my Mistress was sitting rocking yourself in the middle of the floor, and how pleased you were to see them. I was on my way to Mr Clapps to see them when I heard that they had gone to Jonesboro. I believe they did not stay here so long as they intended when they came. The trustees of the academy in Jonesboro I understood wrote to them urging their immediate return. Well now my dear Mistress I must begin to tell you all about home. The house looks exactly as it did when you left it. It has been aired regularly, and every part attended to after a rain or snow. The yard looks very well and has not been injured at all except some of the peach trees in the part of the yard next to the mill dam were some what injured by a deep snow which fell the last of March or first of April. Mr Lathim & Page went as quickly as they could and shook the snow from all the trees or I think they would have been very much injured. It was the deepest snow I have ever seen in this country. We have had a cold and dry spring, and I was afraid that all the fruit was killed, but I hope it is not. I am not a very good judge of such things, but I examined some of the peach blossoms, and think that some of the fruit is safe unless we have more hard frosts. The pine, and all the other trees look well. In the garden aunt Lethe has sowed all the different kinds of vegetable seed she normally puts in when you are at home. The strawberry vines are in full bloom, and promise a good crop of fruit. I should like to know what you would wish done with them. If you wish any preserved, and how many. If you do I will endeavour to do them as nicely as possible. If you have no objection I will sell the ballance, and see how profitable I can make them for you. Aunt Lethe was somewhat annoyed by persons from town, schoolchildren & who crossed the garden, so she put a lock on the gate, and we have determined not to let any one go in it again, unless some lady that we know would not molest any thing. The currants and gooseberries look well, and are tolerably full of fruit. Please let me know if you would wish me to make any currant jelly, and if you would like me to bottle the gooseberries. I would wish you my dear Mistress to give me especial directions about every thing that you want done, and I will if I am spared do as exactly as you wish me as I can. Aunt Lethe says she will try to have what she can in the garden for you when you come, and I will try to have plenty of chickens ready. The old hens you left are still here, and some chickens hatched since you left here we raised in the cellar. I wish you could have seen them. they were all as white as milk and all except one or two that the old cat caught are now laying. I have not very good news to tell about the cows. We have as yet but one young calf, but Aunt Lethe expects several more very soon. She now milks but three cows, but she churns regularly once, sometimes twice a week. Your Florence has a fine beautiful female colt, only a day old, and when I write next I shall tell you I expect of some other addition to the number of colts. Mr Lathim is the most industrious man I ever saw and is as amiable and quiet a young man as ever was. seldom leaves the house. never has left on the sabbath. He seems perfectly contented tho he has no company, but his books on sunday, and during the long winter nights he had a fire in the living room, but always went early to bed, as he worked hard all day. He is very careful and seems to consider your interest in every thing. The whole of Gibsons field even the carriage road is now in corn, and the gate by Mrs Watson's locked up. The meadow next the town entirely to the bars is sowed in oats, which are growing prettily. The greater part of the field at the bottom of the garden is in corn the remainder in potatoes. He has sowed clover in the field next [to] the woods called the well field. The corn is not up but is spouting. Jefferson Washington and even William assisted in planting the corn, and Mr Lathim said they worked as well as Page. I never saw the horses look as fat and well. Mr Lathim feeds and attends to them himself. He rises by day every morning, and stays at the stable until breakfast is ready. Jefferson is becoming quite useful. He assists about the stable, and any other work that Mr L has for him to do. The children are all well except Margaret. She has been quite sick but is now much better. Lucy's youngest is a fine child, not very large, but quite plump. It is the colour of the others. Please tell Eliza that her children look very well. I have not found Mary eating any dirt since she got her mothers letter. Aunt Lethe & Lucy send their love to you & master & miss Virginia & to all the servants. Please give my love to them too. Tell Michael I sent him a letter and his Bible by Theodore who promised to see him and tell him all about us. Mrs Smith set off to Richmond yesterday. Please give my best love to Miss Virginia. I do long to see her more than ever since you told me how well she looked. I have almost filled my paper about ourselves and all at home, but as you desired I must tell you something about your neigh-

bours. Col Whites family is well. Miss Ellen has been
very busy fixing for her trip. Mr Raileys family is well.
Mr R was sick in Philadelphia for some time, but is
expected home today. At Mr Watson's they are all
well. Mr Watson does not stay at home much now,
and Mrs Watson is very lonely since Miss Lucy left
her. She has had several spells of illness since you left
here, has not yet entirely recovered from one she had
some weeks ago. There has been a great deal of
sickness in the country. Mr James Cummings & his
son Robert have been ill but are better now. I hope
sight of Miss Ellen White will be of service to you. I
am anxious to hear which of the servants you intend
taking with you to the north. I hope you will not leave
them in Richmond, particularly David. Aunt Lethe
says she hopes soon to get the letter you promised
her. She was very proud of the one Miss V wrote to
her. I believe I have told you all that you would care
about hearing so I must conclude. I hope I shall soon
hear that you are well again, and shall see you in
August looking as well as ever such is the sincere wish
of your affectionate servant

Hannah [1]

Hannah tells her husband of the pains of separation and
family doings.

Abingdon January 30, 1838

My dear husband

I begin to feel so anxious to hear from you and
my children, and indeed from all the family that I

have concluded to write to you altho you have treated
me badly in not answering my last letter. I heard
through Mr Gibson last week that you were all well,
but hearing from you in that way does not satisfy me.
I want a letter to tell me what you are doing and all
about yourself and Eliza & David. Mr Nat Barker sent
to let me know that he would set off to Richmond in
the stage to day, but I could not get my letter ready in
time for him this morning, but if he has put it off
until the next stage, as I think he probably has I can
still send it by him, or if he has gone, by mail. Mr Watson's Father, Mother, and sister have been staying
with them for some time. His Father & Mother set off
this morning for Charlottesville. Miss Ellen I believe
intends staying with Mrs Railey until the spring. She
has been up to see me several times. Tell Miss
Virginia I wish she was here that she might become
acquainted with her. We have had a very sick family.
Mr Lathum and all the children had the measles at
the same time. They were all very sick for a few
weeks, but not all enough to call in a physician. Mr
Lathum's Father came up and attended to his son's
business while he was sick. There is now a great deal
of sickness in town & country. The measles are still
spreading, and some that have taken cold after having had them are very sick. Our children are very well
and are free from the cough which usually succeeds
the measles. Tell Eliza her children grow very fast.
They do not talk much about her now, but seem to be
very well satisfied without her. I begin to feel anxious
to see you all. I am afraid my patience will be quite
worn out if you do not come back soon. You must
write and tell me when Master talks of returning, and
when you write tell me particularly about Master &

Mistress how they look and if Mistress is as much pleased with Richmond as at first. Let me hear also how Miss Virginia looks and if she likes Richmond as well as Abingdon. I have not heard of any of her friends receiving a letter from her. Whenever I see any of them they make particular enqueries about her, and some of them complain of her not writing to them. Mrs Watson says she is tired of waiting for a letter from her or Mistress, so she intends writing to them soon. Tell Richard I have not heard from his wife since she left here. She promised to write as soon as she was settled. I do not think that Mrs Mayo's friends have heard from her, but we think they must be in Mississippi by this time. Tell Miss Virginia her friends are all well. Miss Ellen White has been very sick. But she is now well and has gone to Smythe to stay a short time. Tell David I am much pleased to hear that he has been a good boy. he must continue to be so, and tell him he must send me a message in your next letter. Give my love to Eliza and tell her she must write to me. I want to hear how she gets along without her Mammy to help her. Give my best love to Master & Mistress and to Miss Virginia. Give my love to Richard & David, and believe me always your affectionate wife

Hannah Valentine [2]

Please give my love to your brothers & sisters and to their wives & husbands. I forgot to tell you that Mrs McVicar left a beautiful Bible as a present for you. I have put it away safely for you until you come. Aunt Lethe & Lucy send their love to you all.

Hannah Valentine

Hannah writes Eliza, another house servant, more about home life.

Abingdon. Nov. 1ˢᵗ 1837

Dear Eliza

I Receved yours & Richards Letter day Before yesterday with great pleasure I have been quite uneaseay since for an opportunity to write to you. You must not expect [me] to write to you Often as it is some trouble to get a person to write for Me—I Have written to Michel by Nancy Singleton. Your Children are all well and doing very well—and have never suffered from sickness one moment since you Left here they talk some Little about you but do not appear to miss you a great deal I am not as well my selfe as I would wish to be although I am still about and do all my Business but am Quite unwell—Your Little Daughter Mary is one of the best Children in the world and is very Little like a child—You must make Miss Virginia Read this Letter over 3 or four times as I Have to get some of the first Cut of young Gentlemen to write them—tell My Dear son Richard that I will Have a few Lines written to Him to day his Wife and Friends are all well. His Wife has not yet Received his Letter but I will try and send it to Her between this and Sunday. Give My best Love to Michel & David tell Michel that I am very Happy to Hear that he Has seen all his Relations tell them all they must behave themselves and be as Genteel as they posibly can and try and take Good care of their Master & Mistress Knowing they are the Best Friends they have in this World. tell David he must be a good Boy as Nothing Will give me as much pleasure as to hear of his Good Conduct and it is all my thought for fear you not conduct your selves as Genteel as I would wish you to do. tell Miss Virginia I will Send Her Cloak by Ginny Robinson in about 4 weeks as it is impossible for me to send it sooner. Give My Love to Mistress & Master Most Particularly and to Miss Virginia & My Good Husband Michel tell him he can form no Idea how much I Have thought of him since he Left this place and how much I have missed him— Aunt Lucinda and Mary Send their Love to you all and to Master, Mistress & Miss Virginia I Have no Strange news to write to you about Our Town more than I Have told you—Theodore Sterricks send his best Love to Richard & Your Selfe and sais Richard Must Kiss Eliza three times for Him. He sais he has no news that will be interesting to you but that he waited on Sam White & Jane Good to be married Last Saturday night James Turner & Sam Calliway join me in Love to you all and will write to you all to day I expect—Mary tells Me to say to Miss Virginia that she must not forget Her but Remember her in her Prairs tell her that our New Station Preacher is Named Winton Late from Wythe Station there has been a Great Revival of Religion her among the Methodists and about 30 Have joined the Church among the Rest was Mr. Craig. & C Mrs Andrew Gilson had a fine Son on Saturday Night Last and they are Both well. Miss Ellen White Received a Letter from Miss Mary Last Monday She was well & Sent her Love to all Masters Servant on the Hill—tell David that Easter send her Love to him and expects to Receive A Letter from him shortly—No More at Present But Remain your Most Affectionate Mother Until Death

Hannah Valentine [3]

Tell Richard that Aunt Lucinda sais she has Dreamed about him several times since he Left Here—

[In left-hand margin:] Give My Love to All Michels Brothers & Sisters & Tell them all to write to Me—tell Richard that Mary sais he must write to Her!

Montcalm April 18th 1838

My dear and much respected Miss Virginia

I was much pleased at receiving your letter and was very highly flattered to think that you in the gay Metropolis so much admired and caressed should still condescend to remember old Aunt Lethe on the re-tired hill of Montcalm and be assured my sweet young mistress that old Aunt Lethe still remembers you with feelings of the utmost respect and esteem—And my Mistress too I am glad to hear she is getting better and that she has not forgotten lowly *me*—I hope she will still live to be a blessing to all of us—

Everything is going on finely and prospers in my hands—The flowers in the garden are putting out and it begins to look like a little paradise and the Calves and the Chickens and the children are all fine and lively—just waiting your return to complete their happiness—

I am sorry that Masters cow has so little manners as to eat Onions—in the City of Richmond too—well what a disgrace! I wish you to tell her that our Mountain Cows are better trained than that—and that if she will come up here we will learn her to be more genteel and not spoil the Governers milk—Tell My Master I think all the world of him and long once more to see his dignified steps up our hill—Tell Mistress I hope I shall soon hear of her recovery and that we long for the time when she will be again here to give her directions and have every thing as it ought to be and as she wants it—We have all done the best we could since she went away but still there is nothing like having a person of sense to dictate—and then if we are obedient every thing goes on smoothly and happy—I try Miss Virginia to be contented at all times and am determined not to let anything make me unhappy, we are taught to resemble our Maker and He is always happy, therefore it is our duty to be happy too—knowing that his divine Providence is over all our changes and that the very hairs of our head are numbered—I feel very happy and my mind is continually aspiring to that heavenly place where all our sorrows will terminate—You say in your letter "that we have a very good lot if we will improve it" I think so too and when we know that our good Lord is Divine Love & Wisdom in its utmost perfection and that, *that* Love and Wisdom is continually exerted for our welfare how grateful, how active, and how obedient, ought we to be and how confident, in all his mercies—Miss Virginia I feel extremely happy when I think what a good Lord & Saviour we have and I feel determined to serve him to the best of my knowledge. You say that "the spring is a bright season and that the hours flit so lightly away we scarcely notice them" And so it is with the spring time of Life—When one is young the days and weeks pass rapidly by and we are surprised when we find them gone. and how apt we are in the buoyant days of youth to forget— that the Autumn of age, and Winter of death, is coming. But I am persuaded it is not so with you—I know that you *do* reflect on *these things*—I know there are a few young persons who are pious as you are and I have a well grounded hope that in all the relations of life you will sustain yourself like a Christian I wish I could hear some of the good preaching you speak of but the good being is every where. he is at Montcalm in the still breath of evening as much as in the "City full" yes he is evry where present—and even condescends to visit old Aunt Lethe's heart—Oh Miss Virginia my heart is so full I know not what to say— Tell Eliza I thank her for her letter and she must take part of this to herself as I think one letter is enough for such a poor creature as me for I can tell you all I am setting very frail—to what I used to be. Oh Master! Oh Mistress! Oh Miss Virginia I want to see you all and Micheal and Eliza and Richard and David and all; my heart is large enough to hold you all—I pray that the Lord will take care of you and keep you from all evil—I hope I have not made too free in any thing I said—I wanted to write as if I was talking to you— With every sentiment of veneration and esteem I remain Your faithfull servant

Lethe Jackson [4]

I have a keg of butter which will be too old to use when you come—if you are willing Mr Lathem thinks

it best to sell it— please to write by the next mail and
say if you wish us to sell it or not. I think it would be
best to sell it—L J

During the Civil War, several slave house servants corresponded with other slaves and their owners, from whom they
had been separated by the cataclysmic military and political
events. Bella, Jimmey, Daniel DeRosset, and William Henry
Thurber were servants owned by a Wilmington, North Carolina,
mercantile and planting family. The DeRossets had taken refuge
from the war in the interior of the state, but left the four slaves
behind in town. Bella and Daniel were, according to records, over
eighty years old, while William and Jimmey were about in their
mid-twenties. Especially important are the slaves' descriptions of
the wartime privations, their religious feelings, and their attitudes toward blacks and whites.

Wilmington nc   oct 3 1862

my Dear mis i Rite you A fuw lines for to let you
knoo how we ar i hav Bin sick all this well But ar gitting Better sore [so] that i can Bee A Bout. Kitty and
[———?] has Bin very sick with the yaller fever for
sevel Days pass and the peaple that she stay with ar
Driving hir out all the time to wurk and she is not
abbel to wurk for she can hadley stand on hir foot she
want you to not to put hir to that man a gain for she is
all mos wurk to Death By them she has suf more than
tung can tel ant Juler is well ant Beller is Bout all the
Boys is well at the pressent time giv my Best Love to
my mother for mee you all mus pray for Wilmington
that the Lord mit hav mercy on us and save us from
the grate Danger ar over us i Bee leves that wee hav

Sinned A ganc the Lord and the Lord ar Whipping us
for et

the fever Dont sem to Bate

Sum Days et stops for A white and then spred A
gain i never saw the Like Bee for of our town ef you
walk in the street et Look Like A sory ful time all Day
long the hurs is going

i have not got time to say en ney more
from you or Bedent / Servent

William Henry [5]

george Beny is very sick with the yaler fever the
Charles[ton] Doctor wus Down to see this mor ning

Wilmington N.C.   Oct 3d 1862

My Dear Afectionate Mistress

i take the present oppotunity of writing you these few
lines hoping they may find you & all the family well as
they leves and every un well i am not egzacly down
but i feels quite weak Juliet is tolarable well she has
bin quite unwell but it better Kitty Ann has bin quite
sick with yellow feaver but she is little better i am
sorry to hear of you all greaf about mas Willie & mas
Army [Armand] i feel very sorry for them give our
love to all the white family & to Marriah & Fanny &
Peggy & tell them if i never see them in this world a

gain i hope to meet them in heaven where parting will
be no more   tell them all they have to do is trust the
lord in his mighty power for he will bring us out more
than [he will] conquer of them that love him   Tell
Marriah she must serve the lord she must not forget
what i told her concerning the lord   Joseph is up at
Mr Parsley Place he has not bin down since the sickly
season he is well George has come home sick while
wee ware writing Jessie has bin quite sick but is better   All the rest of the boys are well   Francis is out of
town i am very much ablige to you for the monney
you sent us   i was glad to Recieve the letter from
you   Provisions are very scerce here & nearly all the
stores are shut up   the town looks lonesome   most all
the peaple has left   there are eight or ten doctors
here from savanah & Charleston & nurses   the
feaver seems not to be quite so bad to day four or five
deths to day & last night all the rest of the boys are
well   Jimmie sends his love to miss Lizie and says he
will get the rossin & send it up as soon as posible Julia
sends her love to miss lizie & miss Mary & the children   The lord is my only Trust to care & keeping i
commend my self   His hands has up held me in my
weekness & has often made me strong & who shall
pluck me from his hands. Julia says she will write to
you and miss lizie as soon as she finds out wheather
George has yellow feaver or not

        Nothing more at Present   i Remain your affec-
tionate servant untill deth

                        Bella DeRosset [6]

[79]

Wilmington nc   oct 23 1862

i Re seve you letter and wus glad to hare from you in
my trubble and i truss that the lord hav kind pray in
my Bee half   i am gitting Better all But A Bad head
ake   i have neve Bin sore sick in my life Bee fore But
the lord has spar my life for sum good purpis i
hope   i hope i will Bee well A nuff to gore to wurk in
A day or sor But Dannel is sore sick that i have to stay
with him he Dont sem to git en ney Better i am a verry
on essey A Bout him ant Beller is A little Better to Day
But Wellington is very Bad off with the fever he wus
talking lass night we call the doctor to him this morn
ning we hav got A nice doctor   he put mee in mine
off my old marster hoo kind he wus to us when we
wus sick or doc is name doc green hoo i hope that the
lord will Bless him for his kind niss to us   ant Juller is
not so well But is up i am looking for hir to Bee doon
But the lord has spare hir to wate on the Rest   i will
try to git A liss of the Dead and send et up when i can
git et sore that you all can see for you self ples send us
sum apples ef you can git them ples direct my letter in
the car of JC Smith i hav not got time to say en ney
more at pressent from you servent

William henry thurber [7]

Wilmington N.C. March 25 / 63

My kind & afectionate Misstress

I hope these few lines may find you well also Miss
Cathrine & the rest of the family   i recieved the note

[80]

you sent me and i have full premishion to marry from
Mr Castin i dont like to have to beg but when i know it
is my own owner from whom i am asking these favors
it promps me to do so & there fore i hope miss Lizzie
you will not look oppon it hard i want to ask you
please mam to send me some monney to try to get
some thing deasent to get married in   i expect to be
married in may if nothing hapens to prevent if yankies
dont bother   now miss Lizzie i have an eye to the times
i know the times is hard & have bin waiting for this time
to Pass but the lord knows best   most all my time is
taken up at the office & i cant make much tho they are
very kind to me at the office & gives me plenty to Eat   i
can find no fault at all i hope you and all will be able to
return home soon in peace & safety   i will try & be
faithfull to you untill you comes home again   the
Reason why i write to you for some monney so soon is
because i want to look a round & see what i can
get   Aunt Julia & aunt Bella sends thier love to
all   alls well i would of write you a longer letter but i
have bin making envelopes at the office so late to night
that i must close goodnight My Dear misstress May
the lord of host be with us and the God of Jacob be our
Refuge

From your affectionate Servant
Jimmey [8]

Wilmington NCa Auguste / 63 th

my Dear mrs a few lines to you and hope and trus that
you are well and all of the famly ar well and hope to
find you the same as thease few lines leaves us at the

presente time and not for get inge your Dear sister
please mam let me no when you all are come inge
home i wuld like to have the pleshure of seinge you all
agen But i be leave that i mus go to Hills boro and
then return home agen you mus not think hard of
me for not riten to you befor my Dear mrstres i have
not neglected you by no meanes i Could not find the
time to rite you a letter and i hope and trus that you
will ex scuse me for thes and all the Boys sends thear
love to you and all of the famly   i am thank full that
you have had me taken away from the danger that i
was disposed of that is cuplin up the Cars and i feal
better satussfyed in my mind at the presente time and
allso thank you and Master kindly for your attention
toward me ante Juliar is a little Better and sends hur
love to you and to hur Dear Missis and hope that she
is well at the presente time Austin jine me in love to
you and hope to find you and all well   he is well at
the presente and Joshua sends love to you and fred
and henry and Brother William and Children   his
Babey is ill and donte seame to get aney better a tall
Cusin gorge sends his love to you and to all the famly
and francis the same and promes

         you mus ex cuse my note

              But Mrs van Sickle
                   Bought Mr [————?] house and
                        lote and is moven in it today

please mam send you letter
to me in care of Mr Wm[————?]
Rail Road agente Wil and Weldon

nothinge more from your truly survente in the
lord   I still remane
          Daniel DeRosset of Wilmington N Ca [9]

i have sum money to send Miss Kathy and donte no
how to send it

CHAPTER
THREE

Artisans and Hirelings

MASTERS TRAINED SLAVE craftsmen for large, self-sufficient plantations, and many slave artisans also worked in towns and cities. Some masters hired out their skilled bondsmen to neighboring farmers or planters, while some artisans were permitted to hire out their own time and to share their earnings with their owners. Of all slaves, artisans were the most highly trained and had the greatest desire to control their own work. They could therefore express their alienation more articulately than most field hands, whose rage more often expressed itself through action than words. Thus artisans filled the ranks of conspiracies and rebellions, and they rarely betrayed planned uprisings. Since their work provided both a large measure of self-esteem and independence, the leadership of slave rebellions naturally gravitated to them.

Letters written by or relating to slave artisans or hirelings are less common than those composed by other elite bondsmen, but a few have survived.

In 1824, Brutus, a slave house-builder who had been permitted to hire himself out, dictated a letter to his master, John Haywood, a wealthy North Carolina planter, explaining his problems in getting work.

Dear Sir

It has been some time since Brutus has forwarded to you any money on account of his hire, and he has requested me, to state to you, the reasons which have prevented him from doing so, for so great a length of time—He had made an engagement in the spring to paint a house for Mrs. Troy of this place, which he expected to have finished, during the summer, but was prevented from continuing the work, for want of Materials, and was unable to get another job at that time, and since the commencement of the fall, he has been quite sick, he has however, entirely recovered, and is now engaged on Mrs. Troys and on Mr. Brown's houses—from these persons he expects to receive at least $100 by Christmas which he promises shall be remitted to you immediately, and I have no doubt but he will be able to do so.—Brutus' business is rather dull here at present, there being but few buildings going on, owing probably to the very great scarcity of money.—I shall advise him after finishing the work now on hand, to go over to the new town of Lexington, where, I think, he will do much better.

Very Sincerely
Yr friend & obt. Servt
Wm. Sneed [1]

Two years later, Nancy Venture Woods, an elderly black woman, probably freed by John Haywood, requested a favor for her grandson.

Newbern [N.C.] Feb 5th 1825

Dear Master

I send my best respects and love to you Mistress
and all the children   tell Miss Betsy [————?] she
promised to send me a luving cup and I have not
forgot her and I hope she still remembers me   Dear
Master I will now inform you about my little family   I have at this time seven in family six grandchildren and one great grand child and I am now a
great grand mother   Virgin is the eldest Nancy the
next who has now become a mother   William Brutus
Venter Jone [Jane] & George is the names of the
children that I have taken care of   Virgin is desires
to be put to a trade and I think it would be the best for
him a tailor or shoemaker would suit him best in
consequence of a hurt he has had in his ancle which
he still feels at times   I had rather keep the rest if
agreeable to you to assist me in supporting the small
ones but I feel willing that you should do by them as
you please   as for my own part I am a good deal
afflicted with the rhumatic pains and I hope dear
Master if I should be the longest liver you will remember your old servant for I wish to end my days in
this place   if I was to be carried from here now it
seems that I could not be satisfied   I also wish to
keep the children as long as I live except such as you
think best to put to a trade

You will please to write to M. Guion concerning
the putting of Virgen to a trade and he will see to the
business   I hope that you and yours may be abun-
tantly blest in this life and in the world to come ever-

lasting life and oh may we all meet in a better world than this is the prayer of your servant

to the best of Masters

Nancy Venture Woods [2]

Another slave hireling tells of his affairs.

Quintus Barber to Mr. Charles P. Howard (at Orange Court House, Virginia), Boshers Dam, Sept. 6, 1840

Dear master — I take this opportunity to in form you that we ar well at this time but I had an a tact of the egger & fever in June & July I was in Richmond the 1st of Augost I expected to See mr moton but he was not at home he nor mr Taler neither I expect to go to Richmond the last of this month and if I cant See them likely I Shall come home if I can be Spared from my buisness it is buisey times but money is hard to come at give my love to Mother & all enquireing frends I rote to her but got no ansur whitch affoards me but litle saisfaction William Sends his respects to all his friends pleas to answer this as Soon as you can and let me hear from you all direct your letter to Quintus Barber to the care of Joseph H. Shultz Richmond Va I will coclude my letter by Subscrbing my name—

Your obedient Servent
Quintus Barber [3]

James Boon, a free black, was born in or near Louisburg, North Carolina, in 1808. At the age of nineteen he was apprenticed to learn carpentry, and he began practicing the trade when he turned twenty-one. By 1834, Boon was hiring other free blacks and slaves as assistants; he soon became well known as a shrewd, skilled contractor in Wilmington, Louisburg, and Raleigh, once even making repairs on a local courthouse. Though Boon was never prosperous, and received somewhat lower wages than whites in the same trade, he did acquire one slave youth, probably for benevolent reasons, to whom he later gave employment.

Boon's wife, Sarah, belonged to a Louisburg woman who lived on a farm near Raleigh, where Boon worked. James and Sarah had one son who apparently worked with his father. Since the family was split up, however, a correspondence developed among its members.

Sarah Boon's sister, Lucy Smith, shares some distressing news.

Fayetteville NC
May 1, 1842

My Dear Sister

We received your letter last Saturdy that contained the distressing news of our dear Mother Death   we did not know untill we received it that she had moved   it gave us grate pleasure to hear that she was with her Daughter when she died   it greved us much to hear that she was no more and to know we should see her no more   but we sorrow not as those who have no hope for we know our loss is her eternal gain   we wanted very much to go up and see her last Christmass but were disappointed   I have nursed Miss Della Baby ever since it was born that was one reason why I could not go   I have no news to tell you   I am glad to hear that times is the same with you as when we were there   the Methodist Preacher Mr Mood Emersed two yesterday in the creek   there was great rejoiseing

   Your Brother sends his love to you   he received your letter but has neglected to answer it   his son garner is married to Jacob Harrises Daughter and has got a son   his health had improved very much   my health is not good   Estra has been in bad health all the winter   your Brother sends his love to you and all your family   give our love to Sister, Brother your Mother husband and all your family. accept a portion for your self   prey for us your Affactionate Sister Lucy Smith ⁴

   Louisburg [NC] November 27th, 1849

my dear husband, I hasten to answer your welcome letter which was received a few days since. Your wishes have been attended to, as far as they were in my power. I sent to mr Hawkins immediately after the reception of your letter to know if he intended to haul the rails he had promised, but he has not done it. I sent also to Mr. Taylor to know if the pen could be put up, but he said it could not be put up now, it would be too much in his way, but that he would leave week after next and then I would do as I pleased, and Jack Shaw said he would buy the rails if Mr Hawkins did not have them hauled before then. I think it would be better for you to come home if you can stay only one day, for your hogs are running wild and I fear they will all be destroyed for I can do nothing.— We are all well at present. Give my love to my son and tell him I hope he is doing well and attends preaching regularly. If you do not intend coming, write soon and let me know what I must do, but I think you had better come if possible.—I remain your devoted wife

Sarah Boon [5]

Troubles with a husband too long away from home—another "worman."

Louisburg July 11, 1850

My Dear Husband

I now address to you these humble lines to informe you that I am well and hope they will find you injoying the same blessing   I was trueley sorey to hear that your health was bad. I wish you to let me no if you should get down sick and I have know doubt but what my owners would let me come and stay with you. As for doubting your word that is a thing that I have never down before. The reason that I had for doubting you word was when the subject was broach before you and that worman eather of you mad no reply. I would have spoken in defiance of any thing for the sake of my wife. when the words were spoken. but let it be eather way. My Dear Husband I frealy forgive. I have no doubt that you will find it in the end that I was rite. I wish it to be banished from our memoreys and it neve to be thought of again and let us take a new start and join on together as we have binn doing for many years. Miss Marian has given t me great concorlation but before that I was hardely able to creep. I hope you will concider my fealings and give me the sentiments of your mind in ancer to this letter. I think it would be better for you to wind up your buisness in Raleigh if you could conveantley and come some where clost about me witch would be a great prise to me than all the money you could make. I have not heard from our little son since he left but expect to hear soon and I will let you know as soon as I can. I wish you to rite me word when you rite when you are coming out. I do not thing it is rite to for me for sutch a long absence from me if I cant come to join you. [You] can come to me. we are all well as to health. I feel very loanesome   be sertin to answer this letter as soon as you get it. I have nothing more at present, onley I remain your Affectnate Wife untill Death

Sarah Boon [6]

PART
TWO

Protest, Escape and Rebellion

TO THE RIGHT HONORABLE WILLIAM, EARL OF DARTMOUTH,
HIS MAJESTY'S SECRETARY OF STATE FOR NORTH AMERICA,
ETC.

Should you, my lord, while you peruse my song,
Wonder from whence my love of Freedom sprung,
Whence flow these wishes for the common good,
By feeling hearts alone best understood,
I, young in life, by seeming cruel fate
Was snatch'd from Afric's fancy'd happy seat:
What pangs excruciating must molest,
What sorrows labour in my parent's breast?
Steel'd was the soul and by no misery mov'd
That from a father seiz'd his babe belov'd:
Such, such my case. And can I then but pray
Others may never feel tyrannic sway?

—*Phillis Wheatley,* Poems on Various Subjects, Religious
and Moral (*1786*)

I left North Carolina august before last and I had god by my side and he helped me a long. I traveled 65 miles and we had 52 in our number. before we crost the river we could whear the pickets soods [swords] strike the stirrup and we taught we wold be taken eny moment the babys cried and we could whear the sound of them on the wanter   we lay all night in the woods and the next day we trabeled and we reached Suffolk that night and we lost twenty one of the Number

—Emma Bynum, describing her escape to Union lines from North Carolina to Suffolk, Virginia, ca. 1863–1865. From H. L. Swint, ed., Dear Ones at Home (1966)

*F*rom the outset, Africans vigorously resisted their enslavement by Europeans. Blacks revolted in the "baracoon" trading depots along the African coast, and uprisings on board slave-trading vessels were not uncommon, most notably in the Amistad and Creole incidents of 1839 and 1841. Once in the New World, slaves opposed servitude by a variety of means, ranging from a "surly look" to spectacular rebellions. Slave insurrections and harassment from maroon colonies containing several thousand runaways plagued the slave societies of Brazil, Jamaica, and Cuba from their inception. In the seventeenth century the runaway colony of Palmares in northwestern Brazil waged a sixty-five-year struggle for autonomy; in the nineteenth century, several decades of uprisings culminated in the Bahía rebellion in 1835. In Jamaica a maroon war lasted from 1730 to 1739, and major slave rebellions occurred in 1760 and 1832. Cuban slavery was not completely abolished until after the racial civil war of 1868–1876. Even more significant was the first successful slave revolt on French Saint-Domingue from 1791 to 1804, which resulted in the establishment of Haiti—the first black republic in the New World.

In North America many bondsmen fought for the independence of the United States with the Colonial armies during the Revolution and the War of 1812, while others escaped to freedom behind British lines. Still others petitioned the government for their liberty on the basis of their military service or the disloyalty of their masters. Many attempted to earn and save enough money to purchase themselves or their families—even though the possibility of making arrangements for manumission declined during the nineteenth century because of increasingly restrictive state legislation.

Slaves appealed in writing for assistance to various antislavery organizations; some even turned to the American Colonization Society for help in returning to their African homeland. When outside organizations proved inadequate, bondsmen and their friends formed the Underground Railroad, the loose escape and communication network that linked the Upper South with the North and with Canada.

Most frequently, plantation slaves expressed their opposition to slavery by refusing to work, performing sloppy work, stealing goods, fighting with their overseers, sabotaging machinery, breaking tools, burning down buildings, or attempting to run away. In addition, slaves resisted the white man's culture and religion. They appropriated what they wanted from Christianity—such as the story of the Israelites and of Christ's suffering—and used it as a source of strength. Spirituals expressed the misery of enslavement and the longing for freedom.

Each year in the last antebellum decades, more than 1,500 slaves successfully escaped to the North, while within the South countless blacks sought permanent refuge in swamps and mountainous regions, or with Indian tribes. From these "maroon" colonies—which had their counterparts in Latin America on a much larger scale—fugitives raided plantation districts and transportation facilities. Accompanied by a band of black and white guerrillas, John Brown planned to use these outcast communities as a base for his invasion of Virginia in 1859.

The most dramatic means of slave resistance, however, were conspiracies and insurrections. Plots and uprisings surfaced with a frequency of at least one major outbreak per generation, which was sufficient to keep whites in periodic states of panic. The most important rebellions occurred in New York City in 1712, in South Carolina in 1739 and 1740, in Richmond, Virginia, in 1800, in Louisiana in 1811 and 1812, in Charleston, South Carolina, in 1822, and in Southampton County, Virginia, in 1831.

Altogether, the various forms of slave resistance suggest that American blacks managed to retain their humanity under dehumanizing conditions, and to confront their masters with an array of ingenious protests. Slaves created a way of life opposed to that which masters desired and perpetuated a tradition of vigorous opposition to oppression.

CHAPTER
FOUR

To Make Free

THROUGHOUT THE SLAVE period, bondsmen attempted to purchase themselves and their families out of bondage by con-
vincing masters to fix a price, finding work, and saving enough
money to compensate their owners. Around the turn of the
nineteenth century, when slavery was not always profitable,
some masters were willing to enter into such arrangements. But
after the 1820's, as the plantation system expanded, state legislatures prohibited slaves from "hiring out their own time" and
refused to recognize manumission. Because of their "bad example" to slaves and their participation in conspiracies like Denmark Vesey's, free blacks were increasingly regarded as a threat
to Southern society, so that whites attempted to prevent self-
purchase and to drive freedmen from the South. Deceitful
masters reneged on self-purchase agreements after slaves had
earned their price, while selfish masters were reluctant to part
with slaves except for outrageous sums of money. The problems
facing slaves who attempted to purchase themselves are revealed
in the letters and petitions of Caesar Brown, Robin Cox, and
Rose Hill.

Nassau N P May 30th 1800

Dear Mistress,

By the death of my laste mistress, which I regret most sincerely, I find myself left your slave, notwithstanding the constant assurances of Mr. Brown my former Master & his wife to the contrary, who really did promise to make me free at their death. All the slaves myself included are to be sold here or sent to you, they have all been apraised at a proper valuation, except me, on whom they have fixed the immoderate price of 500 Dollars. My only motive for intruding this letter on you, is to beg that you will consider my Master's promise which you know to be true, you likewise know with what real fidelity I have served him and his wife, and you must be convinced of my attachment to my young Master & you, indeed I am convinced that you will render me every service in your power & endeavor to make my situation somewhat more independent than it has been hitherto. If it is your wish to have me in New York I will with pleasure go there and serve you forever, but if on the contrary it is your intention I should be sold with the rest of the slaves, I beg you so far to indulge me as to lower the price at which I am valued and I will try to purchase my own freedom, with the assistance of some friends in this place. Master Patrick Brown has promised to advance me a little money towards procuring my emancipation if you chuse to part with me. It is My dear Madam my wish to purchase my freedom and I hope you will have the goodness to consent to it and to moderate the present sum at which I am apraised.

I must pray you to consent to write me your determination—please to enclose your letter to Martin P. Brown.

> I have the Honor
> to be,
> Dear Madam,
> Your Faithful Slave,
> Caesar Brown [1]

    To the Honorable the Speaker and members of the Legislature of Virginia—The memorial and petition of Robin Cox [a black man] of the Town of Petersburg respectfully represents—That during the year 1809 he obtained his friend Jacob Carter [a free black man] to purchase your petitioner of Daniel Dodson Esqr. of said Town [by whom he was raised] for the purpose of giving him his freedom, but your petitioner not being aware of the necessity of applying to your honorable body yet remains in a state of suspence truly pitiable; He has refunded the purchase money to his friend four year since, who is also anxious that your petitioner should enjoy the privileges and immunities of other free persons, as will more fully appear by an instrument of writing given by the said Carter to the said Robin & bearing date 24th July 1810

    Your petitioner prays your honors to take his case into consideration and permit him to reside in his native place, where he has a wife and several children, and enjoy his freedom purchased by his industry & enterprise—and your petitioner as in duty bound will ever pray

> P. Haxall—believes the Petitioner to be honest sober and Industrious. Daniel P. Organ has known for some years the Petitioner and believes him to be honest and industrious.[2]

Two certificates of good character are given and are signed by twenty-one citizens of Petersburg.

Sir I will thank you if you will Speak to Mr Boudinot about the Bisiness Conserning myself and my Master Mr James Sutton as you can see Mr Boudinot at the Bank of the U States Every tuesday and fridays at 10 oClock—if Mr Hartshorn Can get my master to let me pay the money to you I Shall be glad as I can pay 80 Dollars at this time—I should be glad if you Could see Mr Skyren and See my papers   Sir I am the Servant James Carter

> Rose Hill [3]

[On back in different handwriting:]
> See Elias Boudinot about Jas Carters Freedom NB Lives w. E B.

To escape bondage, slaves often turned to their family.

Caldwell June 3d 1805

My dear Son Cato

I long to see you in my old age   I live at Caldwell with Mr. Grover the Minister of that place   now my dear son I pray you to come and see your dear old Mother—Or send me twenty dollar and I will come and see you in Philadelphia—And if you cant come to see your old Mohter pray send me a letter and tell me where you live what family you have and what you do for a living—I am a poor old servant I long for freedom—And my Master will free me if any body will ingage to maintain me so that I do not come upon him—I love you Cato you love your Mother—You are my only son—

This from you affectionates Mother—
Hannah Van Buskerk now—
Hannah Grover [4]

P.S. My dear son I have not seen you since I saw you at Staten *Island* At Addee Barker's 20 years ago—If you send any money send it by Dotr. Bone and he will give it to me—If you have any love for your poor old Mother pray come or send to me   My dear son I love you with all my heart—

Hannah Van buskerk—

Although some masters were reluctant to free their slaves no matter what the compensation, free blacks pressed such slave-holders so they could "get together once More" with their enslaved loved ones.

Greene County Tennessee 26 Fabury 1818

Sir

I Recieved your Letter of the 9 January Stateing
that you was informed that I was the owner of your
Wife Sarah & also whether I would feel Disposed to
part with her to you and also the Terms—The Ties of
Humanity compells me to part with her under these
Serious Circumstances of Restoreing to a Dis-
conselate Husband a Beloved wife—no Sum of
money would induce me to part with Sarah for She is
my princaple dependance in my House and Kitching
as a Servant   She is Sober, industrious & Honest so
much so that my wife always finds her things in
proper order without much Trouble—and as the
Price of Black People is so Enormously High in this
Country that I could not Replace Such a one as her I
Expect for less than Between Six & Seven Hundred
dollars and Such a Trusty one as She is—is hard to
find, and as I observed above a sum of money wuld
not induce me to part with her and as it is Both your
Desiers to be once more united together again, it is
my wish also, & all I want is to Reduce the price as
Low as Possible which will be five Hundred & fifty
dollars   Hopeing that I should be the means of Gratifying Both your Desiers in order that you Should
come together once more to Spend the Ballance of
your days together in Love and Peacefull Harmony &
that price I will Sacrafise fifty dollars at least But that
I will Freely do in order to assist you and her in your
Expenses—I wish you to consider the contents of this
Letter and what Time would sute you the Best to
Redeem her—any Time this Spring or Next Summer

will answer me so as to Sute your Convenience—But I wish you to inform me the verry Time will sute you Best—as I must make my arrangments to Replace one as soon as Shee goes & cannot find my self able to purchase Without the Money as I cannot do without Two, living in Such a Publick Place—State to me the Time that will sute you the Best to Redeem her and then a Strict Compliance to that information will be Expected by your

> Huml. Sarvt.
> James Guthrie [5]

NB Sarah Has Frequently mentioned to her
Mistress that She had lost all Hopes of
Ever Seeing you but Seemed to be Revived in a
Transport of Joy when She heard your letter

James Cooper My dear Husband I was Glad to Hear from you when your Letter Come to hand and that you was well and Had not forgot me my dear Husband Try to Redeem me and I will assist you in Reimbursing the Money so that we may git together once More and Live together the Ballance of Our days I am will and With den   Respect Your Loveing Wife Till Death

> her
> Sarah   X   Cooper [6]
> mark

On a hot July morning in 1853, John Scott led twenty-two of his fellow slaves to the office of the Mayor of Richmond.

There Scott demanded, according to the July 19 *Richmond Enquirer,* "to ascertain from the records, whether or not they had been emancipated by the will of their late master," John Enders. The mayor immediately arrested them, informing the blacks "that they were all slaves, having no claim whatever to freedom; and that if they were again caught at large . . . he would punish each and all with 39 stripes."

Below, Scott details his attempt to gain his freedom.

Richmond Va September 19th 1853

Rev, And Dear Sir,

I wish to inform you that it has been our great & long desires to go to Liberia for a settlement but we could not comply with our wishes on account of not being free at first. Since that time our Master promise to set us free at his death, at which time we expected to obtain our freedom and our Master, old Mr John Enders, has Died very near 2 years ago at which time our freedom was talk about by white gentlemen of this city, and at this time young Mr John Enders, son of the deceased, Said to us be not troubled for he would do all for us that his father had said in the Will, and that we were then working for ourselves, and since that time we have been kept here in bondage, and hire out by the year, and do not get the money that we are hire out for, and we has said and done every thing in our power to get our rights according to the Will of *old* Master, but being Slaves we has not obtain them as yet, and this is the reason you has not heard from us and the reason why we are kept so long from the home of our forefathers in Africa. There is now about 118 in all who has been left free; and we humbly beg you to help us out if you can, if you can undertake for us & advocate our cause we shall be very glad for you to do so, or if you can give us any advice or information how we should act in regard to this matter it will be thanfully received, and you will be rewarded. We have made some 2. or 3. attempts by Lawers to get a copy of the Will, but they has deceived us and got our money, and we are left to grop our way in bondage, fare from Africa the home of our forefathers. Our desire for going to Liberia was on the increase up to last July 19th and they are still on the increase up to this present moment. It was on the 18th of last July that a number of us went to the Court house, to the Clerks office, to hear the Will of our master read, but the officers send us away with a admonition to be still on that subject, but we can not be still untill we get home to Africa. Out of 118 Slaves there is some 45 or 50. of them who can read, and some 6. or 7. who can read & write and one is a very good preacher and the most of us have free wives with many boy children. Dear Sir, you will please send us as many Pamphlets as you can spare at present and when you answer this you will then write us word what the Pamphlets will cost us. The whole of this matter to some extent has gotten out in the public and if you wish to see some of the newspapers of last July the 19th & 20th dates, we will try to send you some as soon as they are wrote for. Our bribed Lawers has gotten some 2. or 3. Copy for us, and one of them seem to contridicts the other, which lead us to think more strongly that we were set free by our good *old* master, Mr John Enders. I will now close my remarks

by requesting you to give us an Answer as soon as
you can

yours most truely
John Scott [7]

Some freedmen, after being re-enslaved by kidnappers,
sought help from groups like the Pennsylvania Abolition Society
of Philadelphia, which was especially active in the early nineteenth century. Slaves corresponded with this organization, describing their efforts to purchase themselves, to forestall sale to
unknown masters, to obtain papers proving their freedom, to
locate and assist lost relatives, and to escape from re-
enslavement.

Augusta 7th July 1824

Mr. Isaac Johnson

Dear Sir   I write you a few lines that you may
know where I am and how I came here. I was kidnapped by Jacob Purnal Joseph Johnson & Ebenezer
Johnson at the Cross Roads the division of Maryland
and Delaware. I am now in Augusta Georgia owned
by John Filpot. I was brought to Georgia by the above
named Johnson's & Sold to Mr. Filpot, myself & two
Children—Mr. Philip Lee I wish also to know where I
am & my two Brothers, Littleton Stevens & his
Brother James please inform them I am in Augusta
Georgia, and how I came here. I once was Free but
now am a slave. I wish to inform you all that I am still
striving to get to Heaven & if I should not see you all

in this world I hope to meet you all in Heaven there to part no more   I hope you are well and I remain the Same yours

Levina Johnson [8]

[Marked July 7, 1824]

Isaac Johnston Father in law to Levina Johnston states,

That Levina Johnsoton was free born on the E Shore of Md. near the Virginia Line & near Daniel Mifflins mill abt. 16 miles from Snow Hill. Her fathers name Littleton & mothers Rachel Stevens, who where also free born James Knox a Taylor, The Millburn Grocer Levin Townsend, Ralph Millburn, John C Handy Clerk of the Court, Mr Dumocks Taylor Edward Knox James Holland Blk Smith, Tho Spence—all living in Snow Hill Knew that Levina was free born.

About 7 or 8 years since Levina married Isaac Johnston, & moved to the Cross roads at the Division line between Md. & Delaware where she was kidnapped & her two children Rachel & James Johnston.

Philip Lee a cold man Uncle to Levina lives in Howard St Baltimore lower end near the Brick Yard is a porter in a grocery store he is acquainted with Levina & those who can testify to her right to freedom

March 30 1826 wrote to William Maloney jr near Denton Maryland, giving him a statement of the above case & requesting him to attend to it [9]

With kidnapping rife, slaves sought to protect themselves by securing proof of their freedom.

Philadelphia August th 10 1817

Mr Beeston

Sir   as I am in A very critical situation at presant un account of my not having A feew Lines from under your hand to protect me from the cunstables hear who are taken up every persan as runaways tha can lay thare hands upon   thare is one Jack Willmer A molatter fellow from Sarsafract neck that Lived with Mr Willmer has reported that I am A runaway in consequence of that I reported my self to the Maor of the City and he in formed me that if any of the officers should take me up that I should come bee foor him but bee shure to write Down to you and get from under your hand an instrument of writing to protect me from any of them. I have monney Du to me at present for my laibour and I am Afeerd to go and get it   I have A grate Desire to come down and Due not think my Self safe in under takeing the Journey   Sir bee so good as to send mee up A few Lines to cirtify that I was your propperty So that I may go in safety and get my monney that is owning to me and come Down to sea you and my children   Bee so good as send up to me by the fiers opportunity wich will bee on tusDays Thurs Days and Satur Days by

[112]

the Mail and Directly your letter to William Anderson
to the Care of Mr David Johns in white horse Alley

Noe more at present But Remain your most
obedent and very humble sarvant
William Anderson [10]

[*Marked:*]
Zebulon Beasten
respecting Wm. Anderson
This paper establishes the freedom of said William if he has been here six months

Other slaves, such as George Moses Horton, tried to earn
enough money to purchase themselves by performing unusual
services. Horton belonged to a Chatham County, North Carolina, master who sometimes permitted him to hire out his own
time at fifty cents per day at the University of North Carolina,
where he learned to read and write and composed letters and
poems for the students. In 1829, with the help of benevolent
whites, Horton published in Raleigh a collection of poems entitled *The Hope of Liberty,* hoping to raise enough money to gain
his freedom and emigrate to Liberia. Even though the book was
reprinted in 1837 by Philadelphia abolitionists as *Poems By A
Slave,* Horton's efforts failed. Finally, when Union troops swept
through North Carolina in April 1865, Horton escaped to their
lines and accompanied a Union general to Philadelphia. There,
about 1868, he published a second book entitled *Naked Genius,*
just before his death.

On Liberty and Slavery [11]

Alas! and am I born for this,
To wear this slavish chain?
Deprived of all created bliss,
Through hardship, toil and pain!

How long have I in bondage lain,
  And languished to be free!
Alas! and must I still complain—
  Deprived of liberty.

Oh, Heaven! and is there no relief
  This side the silent grave—
To soothe the pain—to quell the grief
  And anguish of a slave?

Come Liberty, thou cheerful sound,
  Roll through my ravished ears!
Come, let my grief in joys be drowned,
  And drive away my fears.

Say unto foul oppression, Cease:
  Ye tyrants rage no more,
And let the joyful trump of peace,
  Now bid the vassal soar.

Soar on the pinions of that dove
  Which long has cooed for thee,
And breathed her notes from Afric's grove,
  The sound of Liberty.

Oh, Liberty! thou golden prize,
  So often sought by blood—
We crave thy sacred sun to rise,
  The gift of nature's God!

Bid Slavery hide her haggard face,
  And barbarism fly:
I scorn to see the sad disgrace
  In which enslaved I lie.

Dear Liberty! upon thy breast,
  I languish to respire;

And like the Swan unto her nest,
   I'd to thy smiles retire.

Oh, blest asylum—heavenly balm!
   Unto thy boughs I flee—
And in thy shades the storm shall calm,
   With songs of Liberty!

The Slave's Complaint [12]

Am I sadly cast aside,
On misfortune's rugged tide?
Will the world my pains deride
            For ever?

Must I dwell in Slavery's night,
And all pleasure take its flight,
Far beyond my feeble sight,
            For ever?

Worst of all, must Hope grow dim,
And withhold her cheering beam?
Rather let me sleep and dream
            For ever!

Something still my heart surveys,
Groping through this dreary maze;
Is it Hope?—then burn and blaze
            For ever!

Leave me not a wretch confined,
Altogether lame and blind—
Unto gross despair consigned,
            For ever!

Heaven! in whom can I confide?
Canst thou not for all provide?

Condescend to be my guide
For ever:

And when this transient life shall end,
Oh, may some kind, eternal friend
Bid me from servitude ascend,
For ever!

Even more fascinating than Horton's poetry, perhaps, is a letter from a slave to a prominent white preacher of North Carolina protesting—with great insight into contemporary economic, social, and racial relations—religious discrimination against Southern blacks.

Wayne County, Ga., 26 June 1821

Master John   I want permition if you pleas to speak A few words to you—I hope you will not think me too bold sir, I make my wants known to you because you are, I believe, the oldist and most experienced that I know of   in the first place I want you to tell me the Reson you allways preach to the white folks and keep your back to us. is it because they sit up on the hill we have no chance a mong them there must we be for goten because we cant get near enoughf without geting in the edg of the swamp be hind you. we have no other chance because your stand is on the edg of the swamp, if I should ask you what must I do to be saved, perhaps you would tel me   pray let the bible be your gide   this would do very well if wee could read   I do not think there is one in fifty that can read   but I have been more fortunate than the most of the black people   I can read and write in my way as to be understood I hopes   I have a weak mind

about the dutys of religious people   If god sent you
to preach to siners did he direct you to keep your face
to the white folks constantly or is it because they give
you money · if this is the cause we are the very persons that labor for this money but it is handed to you
by our masters   did god tell you to have your meeting housis just larg enoughf to hold the white folks
and let the black people stand in the sone and rain as
the brooks in the field   we are charged with inaten-
tion it is imposibal for us to pay good attention with
this chance   in fact some of us scars think we are
preached to at all   money appears to be the object   we are carid to market and sold to the highest
bider never once inquire whither you sold to a
heathon or christian if the question was put did you
sel to a christian what would be the answer   I cant tel
what he was gave me my prise thats all was interested
in   Is this the way to heavin if it is there will [be] a
good meny go there   if not there chance will be bad
for there can be many witnesses against them   If I
understand the white people they are praying for
more religion in the world   oh may our case not be
forgoten in the prairs of the sincear   I now leave it to
you and your aids to consider   or I hope you will
reade it to the chearch   if you think proper   it is
likely I never will hear from you on this subject as I
live far from you   I dont wish you to take any of
these things to your self if nothing is due   do your
god justis in this case and you will doo me the same [13]

CHAPTER
FIVE

Escape to Freedom

W HEN OPPORTUNITIES AROSE, slaves attempted to escape from bondage, and a small but active minority of bondsmen occasionally succeeded. Although most were able to remain absent for only a few days, others managed to stay out for months or years before being caught or forced to return out of desperation for food and shelter. Permanent escape from the South was easiest from the border areas, from which slaves made their way through dangerous territory—slave and free—to relative safety near the Great Lakes or in Canada. Contrary to popular mythology, the initiative for escape always rested with the slaves themselves; by the 1850's the Underground Railroad was well organized with Quakers, abolitionists, and, especially, Northern free blacks helping slaves along their way to freedom.

The motivations of runaways were varied, but they usually included a desire to avoid the drudgery and hardships of work routines, to escape punishment or personal humiliation by whites, and to visit families and loved ones. No matter what the reasons for flight, runaways deprived the South of valuable and skilled workers and added to the potential number of black resisters in the North. Letters by runaway slaves before they reached freedom are extremely rare; those few that survive, however, reveal the motivations of fugitives, their mistrust of whites, the strength of their family ties, and the depth of their religious feelings. Anthony Chase, for example, belonged to a Baltimore widow who refused to permit him to purchase his freedom. Instead, she hired him out to Jeremiah Hoffman, to whom Chase wrote a letter of explanation after his escape.

August 8th, 1827

Sir

    I know that you will be astonished and suprised when you becom acquainted with the unexspected course that I am now about to take, a step that I never had the most distant Idea of takeing, but what can a man do who has his hands bound and his feet fettered He will certainly try to get them loosened by fair and Honorable means and if not so he will ceartainly get them loosened in any way that he may think the most adviseable. I hope Sir that you will not think that I had any faoult to find of you or your family no sir I have none and I could of lived with you all the days of my life if my conditions could of been in any way bettered which I intreated with my mistress to do but it was all in vain She would not consent to any thing that would melorate my condition in any shape of measure So I shall go to sea in the first vesel that may ofer an oppertunity and as soon as I can acumulate a sum of money suficent I will Remit it to my mistress to prove to her and to [the] world that I dont mean to be dishonest but wish to pay her every cent that I think my servaces is worth I have served her 11 years faithfully and think it hard that I offered $5.00 what I was valued at 4 years ago and also to pay 4 per cent until the whole sum was payed which I believe I could of done in 2 years and a half or 3 years at any rate but now as I have to Runaway like a crim-

nal I will pay her when I can   Though I am truly
sorry that I must leave you in the situation that I do,
but I will Recomend to you as a Servant Samuel
Brown that I think a good & honest man and one that
is acquainted well with his business but you can Refer
to Mrs Snyder who is well acquainted with him and
has lived in the hous with him. as my mistress is not in
Town I [have] taken the Last months wages to defray
my exspenses but that money and the five dollars that
you lent me the day before I left you I shall ceartainly
Return before I ship for the sea. I dont supose that I
shall ever be forgiven for this act but I hope to find
forgiveness in that world that is to com. I dont take
this step mearly because I wish to be free but because
I want to do justice to myself and to others and also to
procure a liveing for a family a thing that my mistress
would not let me do though I humblely Requested
her to let me do so

Before I was married I was Promised my freedom then after finding this Peace of writeing which
you will find incloesed I was then confident that I was
free at Mr Williams Death, and so I married   I must
now beg for your forgiveness and at the same time
pray to god for your helth and happyness as well as
that of your family

I am Sir your most Obedient Servt &c
Anthony Chase [1]

PS. People will say that my wife has persuaided me to
this but I so declare that she is inocent of any thing of
the kind and was always oppoesed to any thing of the
kind. AC.

CHAPTER
SIX

Rebellion

THE MOST FASCINATING forms of slave resistance are the conspiracies and rebellions which surfaced in America from generation to generation. Despite savage suppression by whites, blacks continued to conspire, and one historian has catalogued over 200 insurrections, plots, and rumors of disturbances involving ten or more slaves around the beginning of the nineteenth century. Given the brutality of American slavery, the underlying cause of revolt should be obvious, although the immediate precipitants differed from rebellion to rebellion. Still open to study are the origins and backgrounds of the leaders and participants, the various tactics and strategies pursued, and the ideologies set forth.

It is quite certain that most rebellions were led by skilled slave artisans and that urban slaves—especially "industrial" workers and day laborers—were quite prone to insurrection, as the Gabriel and Vesey affairs demonstrate. Even though the problems of organization and communication were more difficult, rural revolts could reach serious proportions, as in Louisiana in 1811–1812 and in Southampton County, Virginia, in 1831. Slave preachers like Goomer the Conjurer, Gullah Jack, and Nat Turner also made excellent leaders. Free blacks did not seem to play important leadership roles until the Vesey conspiracy of 1822, but slaves born in Africa or the Caribbean played leading roles in revolts, as did those American-born slaves who managed to retain much of their African cultural identity. Poor whites were often suspected of participation, as indicated in the record of the Vesey trials and the Dyson Conspiracy, but their actual involvement is still a moot question.

Concerning the strategies of revolt, it is questionable whether the evidence supports one scholar's attempt to categorize them as "systematic," "vandalistic," or "opportunistic." But the tactics in most rebellions are quite clear: they depended heavily upon secrecy, surprise attack (usually at night or on holidays), and support from slaves in nearby areas. The plan usually was to kill all white people—women and children included—starting with the master class; to burn buildings; to capture arsenals, storehouses, and government buildings; and sometimes to expropriate banks and treasuries. As whites were subduing fires in one place they would be attacked, and the arson would be spread to other parts of town.

Rebels often recognized certain whites as potential allies. Quakers, Methodists, or other abolitionist-leaning whites were sometimes singled out; and when the United States was in conflict with European powers, conspirators sometimes designated Englishmen or Frenchmen as friendly. Indians, poor whites, and free mulattoes were also regarded as possible supporters. Rebels seem to have attempted to gain additional recruits outside their base of operations, and presumably tried to stage simultaneous uprisings in several regions. But Nat Turner seemed content to recruit along his line of march, letting his deeds serve to attract other blacks.

Beyond local liberation or the establishment of a black state, rebel strategies are less clear. Few plans were disclosed about what would happen after a city or area was seized—except "full possession of the whole country in a few weeks." On the other hand, rebels had contingency plans for escape: Vesey planned to sail for Haiti or (uniquely) for Africa; Turner seemed headed for refuge in the Dismal Swamp; and other insurrectionaries seemed to have aimed to fight their way to freedom in Spanish Florida, Mexico, or Canada.

A few rebellions achieved an extraordinarily rich ideology beyond the general antiwhite attitudes. The Gabriel rebels blended the biblical story of the Israelites with some knowledge of the black revolution in Saint-Domingue; they also planned to make a silken flag bearing the motto "Death or Liberty," a slogan familiar to all Virginians. Religion became important again in 1812 when "the negroes in the neighborhood said . . . that God Almighty had sent them a little Hell for the white people. . . ." Vesey astutely combined Old Testament tales, African religious rites, communications with Haiti, and knowledge of the antislavery speeches in the congressional debates over Missouri. Nat Turner seemed to rely almost entirely on Christian mysticism to motivate his followers; but his personality was apparently so charismatic that he felt little need to discuss previous insurrections, David Walker's *Appeal to the Coloured Citizens of the World* (1829), or the growing abolitionist movement in the North.

The evidence of conspiracies and insurrections consists in letters to and from rebels, letters by informers, forced confessions and testimony taken in court, and petitions for clemency. The reliability of some of these documents is questionable, and the alleged "voluntary" confessions must be used cautiously. But the available evidence by slaves for the Virginia disturbances of 1800–1802, unrest at the time of the War of 1812, the Vesey plot of 1822, and Nat Turner's rebellion of 1831 deserves further scholarly study.

THE GABRIEL CONSPIRACY OF 1800

DURING THE SUMMER of 1800, Gabriel—a twenty-four-year-old, six-feet-two-inch slave artisan belonging to Thomas Prosser of Henrico County, Virginia—organized a large-scale conspiracy. Gabriel attracted followers from plantations, tobacco factories, and coal mines in the area, sometimes even recruiting at weekend barbecues. The number of blacks involved ranged into the thousands. Inspired by the biblical story of the Israelites, the rebels also believed they had "as much right to fight for liberty as any man." Gabriel planned to kill his master and white neighbors first, then seize arms and capture Richmond (where more arms, supplies, and money could be obtained), and ultimately "take the country." All of the whites were to be "indiscriminately massacred"—"except the Quakers, the Methodists, and the Frenchmen," who were to be spared because they were considered "friendly to liberty." Some "Frenchmen" were allegedly involved, the Catawba Indians were to be contacted for support, and Gabriel "expected the poor white people would also join him." Indeed, the authorities feared that Gabriel might receive help from slaves belonging to Haitian émigrés in Virginia.

On August 30, the night before the revolt was to begin, someone betrayed Gabriel, and a heavy rainfall made the roads to Richmond impassable to the revolutionaries. Later Gabriel attempted to escape by sea but was captured. In September and October, Gabriel and about thirty-five other conspirators were tried and executed, while many others were transported out of the state.

Of the North American slave insurrections, the Gabriel conspiracy remains the least known. Recent collections of documents have appeared on the New York rebellion of 1741, the Vesey plot, the Turner and Louisiana revolts. Presented below are some of the documents from the Gabriel conspiracy trial.

Confession of Solomon [1]

Communications made to the subscribers by Solomon, the property of Thomas H. Prosser, of Henrico, now under sentence of death for plotting an insurrection.

My brother Gabriel was the person who influenced me to join him and others in order that (as he said) we might conquer the white people and possess ourselves of their property. I enquired how we were to effect it. He said by falling upon them (the whites) in the dead of night, at which time they would be unguarded and unsuspicious. I then enquired who was at the head of the plan. He said Jack, alias Jack Bowler. I asked him if Jack Bowler knew anything about carrying on war. He replied he did not. I then enquired who he was going to employ. He said a man from Caroline who was at the siege of Yorktown, and who was to meet him (Gabriel) at the Brook and to proceed on to Richmond, take, and then fortify it. This man from Caroline was to be commander and manager the first day, and then, after exercising the soldiers, the command was to be resigned to Gabriel. If Richmond was taken without the loss of many men they were to continue there some time, but if they sustained any considerable loss they were to bend their course for Hanover Town or York, they were not decided to which, and continue at that place as long as they found they were able to defend it, but in the event of a defeat or loss at those places they were to endeavor to form a junction with some negroes which, they had understood from Mr. Gregory's overseer, were in rebellion in some quarter of the country. This information which they had gotten from the overseer, made Gabriel anxious, upon which he applied to me to make scythe-swords, which I did to the number of twelve. Every Sunday he came to Richmond to provide ammunition and to find where the military stores were deposited. Gabriel informed me, in case of success, that they intended to subdue the whole of the country where slavery was permitted, but no further.

The first places Gabriel intended to attack in Richmond were, the Capitol, the Magazine, the Penitentiary, the Governor's house and his person. The inhabitants were to be *massacred, save those who begged for quarter and agreed to serve as soldiers with them. The reason why the insurrection was to be made at this particular time was, the discharge of the number of soldiers, one or two months ago, which induced Gabriel to believe the plan would be more easily executed.*

Given under our hands this 15th day of September, 1800.

Gervas Storrs,
Joseph Selden.

On September 16, 1800, Ben, alias Ben Woolfolk, was sentenced to death for conspiracy and insurrection. However, he confessed the next day, received a pardon from the governor the day after that, and later testified against other blacks—suggesting the clemency awaiting those slaves who assisted state authorities.

Confessions of Ben alias Ben Woolfolk [2]

The first time I ever heard of this conspiricy was from Mrs. Ann Smith's George; the second person that gave me information was Samuel alias Samuel Bird, the property of Mrs. Jane Clarke. They asked me last spring to come over to their houses on a Friday night. It was late before I could get there; the company had met and dispersed. I inquired where they were gone, and was informed to see their wives. I went after them and found George; he carried me and William (the property of William Young) to Sam Bird's, and after we got there he (Sam) enquired of George if he had any pen and ink; he said no—he had left it at home. He brought out his list of men, and he had Elisha Price's Jim, James Price's

Moses, Sally Price's Bob, Denny Wood's Emanuel. After this George invited me to come and see him the next night, but I did not go. The following Monday night William went over and returned with a ticket for me; likewise one for Gilbert. The Thursday night following, both George and Sam Bird came to see me. Bowler's Jack was with us. We conversed untill late in the night upon the subject of the meditated war. George said he would try to be ready by the 24th of August, and the following Sunday he went to Hungry meeting-house to enlist men. When I saw him again he informed me he had enlisted 37 men there. The Sunday after he went to Manchester, where he said he had recruited 50-odd men. I never saw him again untill the sermon at my house, which was about three weeks before the rising was to take place. On the day of the sermon, George called on Sam Bird to inform how many men he had; he said he had not his list with him, but he supposed about 500. George wished the business to be deferred some time longer. Mr. Prosser's Gabriel wished to bring on the business as soon as possible. Gilbert said the summer was almost over, and he wished them to enter upon the business before the weather got too cold. Gabriel proposed that the subject should be referred to his brother Martin to decide upon. Martin said there was this expression in the Bible, delays breed danger; at this time, he said, the country was at peace, the soldiers were discharged, and the arms all put away; there was no patroling in the country, and that before he would any longer bear what he had borne, he would turn out and fight with his stick. Gilbert said he was ready with his pistol, but it was in need of repair; he gave it to Gabriel, who was to put it in order for him. I then spoke to the company and informed them I wished to have something to say. I told them that I had heard in the days of old, when the Israelites were in service to King Pharoah, they were

taken from him by the power of God, and were carried away by
Moses. God had blessed him with an angel to go with him, but
that I could see nothing of that kind in these days. Martin said
in reply: I read in my Bible where God says if we will worship
Him we should have peace in all our land; five of you shall
conquer an hundred, and a hundred a thousand of our
enemies. After this they went on consultation upon the time
they should execute the plan. Martin spoke and appointed for
them to meet in three weeks, which was to be of a Saturday
night. Gabriel said he had 500 bullets made. Smith's George
said when he was done with the corn he would then go on to
make as many cross-bows as he could. Bowler's Jack said he
had got 50 spiers or bayonets fixed at the end of sticks. The
plan was to be as follows: We were all to meet at the briery spot
on the Brook; 100 men were to stand at the Brook bridge;
Gabriel was to take 100 more and go to Gregory's tavern and
take the arms which were there; 50 more were to be sent to
Rocketts to set that on fire, in order to alarm the upper part of
the town and induce the people to go down there; while they
were employed in extinguishing the fire Gabriel and the other
officers and soldiers were to take the Capitol and all the arms
they could find and be ready to slaughter the people on their return from Rocketts. Sam Bird was to have a pass as a free man
and was to go to the nation of Indians called Catawbas to per-
suade them to join the negroes to fight the white people. As far
as I understood all the whites were to be massacred, except the
Quakers, the Methodists, and the Frenchmen, and they were
to be spared on account as they conceived of their being
friendly to liberty, and also they had understood that the
French were at war with this country for the money that was
due them, and that an army was landed at South Key, which
they hoped would assist them. They intended also to spare all
the poor white women who had no slaves.

The above communications are put down precisely as

delivered to us by Ben, alias Ben Woolfolk. Given under our hands this 17th day of September, 1800.

> *Gervas Storrs,*
> *Joseph Selden.*

On October 9, 1800, the Henrico County Court sentenced Jack Bowler, a slave belonging to William Bowler, to death for conspiracy and insurrection, and ordered him to be hung in November.

Testimony given in the Trial of Jack Bowler [3]

Prosser's Ben.—*The witness deposes that Gabriel informed him that the prisoner was the first person from whom he received information of the insurrection intended by the negroes, which was to centre at William Young's. The prisoner said at the Blacksmith shop, in which the witness worked, that he would raise and enlist men and contend for command with Gabriel.*

The prisoner came to the shop at sundry times, and had frequent conversations and mentioned at repeated times there, that he had procured six or seven pounds of powder for the purpose of fighting the white people: The prisoner agreed (in hearing of the witness) together with Gabriel and Solomon, to commence the fight with scythe blades, until they could procure arms from the white people. He saw the prisoner at his Master's great-house on the Saturday night appointed for the commencement of the insurrection, in company with Gabriel and Solomon, who said and concluded that the excessive bad weather would prevent the people from meeting that night, and appointed the ensuing Sunday night as the time of meeting at his Master's tobacco house; he also saw them together on the Sunday morning following.

Mrs. Prices John.—*I saw the prisoner at Mr. Young's spring, in company with Gabriel: he enlisted with Gabriel and engaged to get as many men to join as he could, and meet in three weeks from that time for the purpose of fighting the white people. Prosser's Tavern being appointed the place of Rendezvous, the prisoner enquired of Gabriel what he was to do for arms: the prisoner applied to many who had agreed to engage in the insurrection, to give him the voice for General. But upon the votes being taken, Gabriel had by far the greater number. Whereupon, it was concluded that the prisoner should be second in command, to-wit, a captain of light horse. The prisoner and Gabriel had secret conversations. Then the meeting was interrupted by the appearance of Mr. Young's overseer, and thereupon the people dispersed, having previously agreed to meet at Mr. Moore's school-house, where a final conclusion on the business should be had.*

Prosser's Sam.—*This witness was a run-away at the time the affair was to have happened: On the Tuesday night of the week appointed for the meeting of the negroes, the prisoner fell in company with a negro by name Frank: the prisoner enquired of the deponent, if he had heard that the negroes were going to rise in arms and fight for their liberty, (being the first knowledge he had of the insurrection,) and the prisoner said the business would certainly commence on Saturday night then next ensuing, if it did not rain hail stones. The prisoner said they intended to sieze on some arms deposited at Priddy's Tavern: a negro by name Charles, having promised to conduct them to the spot where they were kept. In a conversation with the prisoner in the corn field, he remarked that he had procured as much ammunition as two persons could carry, and throwing his arms around Lewis, another negro present, said we have as much right to fight for our liberty as any men: and that on Saturday night they*

would kill the white people; that they would first kill Mr.
Prosser and the neighbors, and then proceed to Richmond.

In late September, Gabriel was captured near Richmond as
he attempted to escape by sea. He was armed with a bayonet
fixed on a stick, which he threw into the river. He claimed he was
a freedman, but could not produce any proof. When captured,
Gabriel promised to confess only to Governor James Monroe,
and those appointed to take his confession reported that "he appeared to make no confession worth reporting." Gabriel was
lodged in a separate cell in the penitentiary, guarded by fifteen
to twenty men at all times, and forbidden to converse with anyone. When Monroe finally interrogated Gabriel, he "seemed to
have made up his mind to die, and to have resolved to say but
little on the subject of the conspiracy."

On October 6, a Henrico County Court convicted Gabriel
of conspiracy and insurrection, and condemned him to execution the next day.

The Trial of Gabriel [4]

Prosser's Ben—Gabriel was appointed Captain at first
consultation respecting the Insurrection, and afterwards
when he had enlisted a number of men was appointed Gen-
eral. That they were to kill Mr. Prosser, Mr. Mosby, and all
the neighbors, and then proceed to Richmond, where they
would kill everybody, take the treasury, and divide the money
amongst the soldiers; after which he would fortify Richmond
and proceed to discipline his men, as he apprehended force
would be raised elsewhere to repel him. That if the white peo-
ple agreed to their freedom they would then hoist a white
flag, and he would dine and drink with the merchants of the
city on the day when it should be agreed to.

Gabriel enlisted a number of negroes. The prisoner

went with the witness to Mr. Young's to see Ben Woolfolk, who was going to Caroline to enlist men there. He gave three shillings for himself and three other negroes, to be expended in recruiting men.

The prisoner made the handles of the swords, which were made by Solomon. The prisoner shewed the witness a quantity of bullets, nearly a peck, which he and Martin had run, and some lead then on hand, and he said he had ten pounds of powder which he had purchased. Gabriel said he had nearly 10,000 men; he had 1,000 in Richmond, about 600 in Caroline, and nearly 500 at the Coal pits, besides others at different places, and that he expected the poor white people would also join him, and that two Frenchmen had actually joined, whom he said Jack Ditcher knew, but whose names he would not mention to the witness. That the prisoner had enlisted nearly all the negroes in town as he said, and amongst them had 400 Horsemen. That in consequence of the bad weather on Saturday night, an agreement was made to meet at the Tobacco House of Mr. Prosser the ensuing night. Gabriel said all the negroes from Petersburg were to join him after he had commenced the Insurrection.

Mr. Price's John—He saw the prisoner at a meeting, who gave a general invitation to the negro men to attend at the Spring to drink grog. That when there he mentioned the Insurrection, and proposed that all present should join them in the same, and meet in 3 weeks for the purpose of carrying the same into effect, and enjoined several of the negroes then present to use the best of their endeavors in enlisting men, and to meet according to the time appointed.

Ben. Woolfolk—The prisoner was present at the meeting at Mr. Young's, who came to get persons to join him to carry on the war against the white people. That after meeting they adjourned to the Spring and held a consultation, when it was concluded that in 3 weeks the business should commence. Gabriel said he had 12 dozen swords made, and had worn out 2 pair of bullet moulds in running bullets, and pulling a third pair out of his pocket, observed that was nearly worn out. That Bob Cooley and Mr. Tinsley's Jim was to let them into the Capitol to get the arms out. That the lower part of the Town towards Rocketts was to be fired, which would draw forth the citizens (that part of the town being of little value); this would give an opportunity to the negroes to seize on the arms and ammunition, and then they would commence the attack upon them. After the assembling of the negroes near Prosser's, and previous to their coming to Richmond, a company was to be sent to Gregorie's Tavern to take possession of some arms there deposited. The prisoner said, at the time of meeting the witness at Mr. Young's, that he had the evening before received six Guns—one of which he had delivered to Col. Wilkinson's Sam. That he was present when Gabriel was appointed General and Geo. Smith second in command. That none were to be spared of the whites except Quakers, Methodists, and French people. The prisoner and Gilbert concluded to purchase a piece of silk for a flag, on which they would have written "death or Liberty," and they would kill all except as before excepted, unless they agreed to the freedom of the Blacks, in which case they would at least cut off one of their arms. That the prisoner told the witness that Bob Cooley had told him if he would call on him about a week before the time of the Insurrection he would untie the key of the room in which the arms and ammunition were kept at the Capitol and give it to him, or if he did not come, then on the night of the Insurrection being commenced, he would hand him arms out as fast as he could arm his men, and that he had on a Sunday previous to this, been shown by Cooley every room in the Capitol.

The Trial of Ben alias Ben Woolfolk, Belonging to P. Grayham [5]

Mrs. Price's John Deposes: That about four weeks ago he saw the prisoner at Mr. Young's Spring. He enlisted with Gabriel to fight the white people, and promised to meet in three weeks, or thereabouts, for that purpose. Gabriel observed, we must slay them as we go; he, the prisoner, said he would do so. He was to have the title and command of Captain.

Prosser's Ben deposes: That he went with Gabriel on a Friday night to Mr. Young's to see Ben Woolfolk whom they found in bed: that he was waked by Sawney and got up. Gabriel gave him money to buy liquor to treat with in Caroline, whither he was shortly going to induce negroes in Caroline to enlist; he expected that he had already six hundred enlisted: he also told Gabriel that he had then six scythe blades in his room, which were to be made into swords by Gabriel, and was about to bring them out, which was prevented by its being inconvenient to Gabriel to carry them with him. That day fortnight, Ben Woolfolk was to meet about midnight at Prosser's Tavern, as he expected he could arrive there by that time with his men from Caroline. Gabriel said they would slay the white males from the cradle upwards, but the females of all ages were to be spared. The prisoner very readily agreed that this was the only way. (Condemned and full confession made.)

SLAVE INFORMERS

Contrary to popular mythology, slave informers came from different backgrounds, not simply from the house-servant group. Indeed, Vesey intended to rely on some "trusted" domestics to slit their masters' throats and to poison Charleston's wells, while at least one "servant girl" assisted Nat Turner's band. But "favorite" servants and "privileged" slaves generally were not dependable, as is indicated by the petition of Louis Bolah and the letter of Poor Black Sam.

On December 6, 1824, in a petition to the Virginia legislature, a Negro named Lewis Bolah explained how in 1812 he had betrayed a slave conspiracy in Louisiana. Ostracized by the black community of New Orleans, the informer sought permission to reside in Virginia. Bolah's petition was supported by several distinguished whites, and his plea was granted.

To the Senate and House of Delegates of the Commonwealth of Virginia—

Your Petitioner Lewis Bolah now a free man of colour but formerly a Slave asks permission most respectfully to represent to the Legislature of Virginia—That he is a Native of this State and resided in the vicinity of the City of Richmond the greater part of his life. That some years past in consequence of the pecuniary embarrassments of his former owner he was sold and transported to the State of Louisiana and became the property of Mr. Waters Clarke of the City of New Orleans with whom he lived for some time. During the year 1812 the slaves and free persons of colour in the City of New Orleans and the surrounding Country connected with a few abandoned and lawless white persons who were bent on rapin and plunder meditated and planed a Plot of Treason and Insurrection which if it had been carried into operation would have presented one general scene of conflagration, murder and robbery & the City of New Orleans and the sorrounding Country if possible would have exhibited a spectacle of ruin and desolation exceeding anything which formerly transpired in St Domingo. This horrible conspiracy was communicated to him, he was invited to join in it, was offered the post of Captain in the operations and assured of being rewarded by freedom and Wealth. Shocked by the proposition and being much attached to his master and family who had treated him most humanely your Petitioner resolved to pursue such a course of conduct as was calculated to prevent the effusion of blood, to bring the ringleaders to trial and punishment and thereby save the lives not only of the whites but the misguided persons of his own colour who might be persuaded to join the nefarious conspiracy and subject themselves to retributive justice and the vengeance of offended Law. He therefore immediately communicated the intelligence which he had received to the Civil Authorities of New Orleans who adopted such plans as caused the apprehension of the ringleaders of the insurrection when assembled in counsel on the very eve of the execution of their Plot and they were condemned and executed—[6]

After the War of 1812 began, Poor Black Sam warned the Virginia authorities that Richmond's blacks were planning a revolt in conjunction with British spies. Though the conspirators had threatened him if he informed, Sam claimed that he had a good master and loved all of the whites.

[Addressed:] To the Governer and Councill aney massa that pick up this will please send it to Cappatoll

Richmond 18th 1812

My Dear m[a]ster   [De]Struction wats Richmon town on 25 nite of Dis mont all the niggros will Rise on that nite to meet in this place   tha mean fost to [as]sa[i]l the Cappitoll and take all the arms   tha got powder nuff and has got maney guns & cut hid thro all dese pine woods Round town   But that will not lead me in to it tha wish me to gine them   But I got good master and love all the white peoples   tha made me sware that I would not tell what tha told me Befor tha told me the Cecret and iffen I will not gine them my life was to Be [de]stroyed if I told it for sur   Dar not make this known so as my name is to be born to lite or deth will be my fate By the Blacks   But will put you all on gard to prepare for that fatall nite   the sceen of the Play House will not be compard with the seen of the nite of the 25 without your gard is Duble and the Drums and fifs in Ratling thro the streets that negers is feard of and lite [your] Houses
    thare is one Inglish Spy live with Moncur at Vander effis next to be Corner but is [dis]Rupting the niggres and tels them that as soon as this pact is made the Inglish will land and then tha all will be free   thar is [a]nother Inglish man in Petersburg doing the same thing   thare is now a cask of Powder plast under the Bank to blow it up and tha will not spair man woman

nor Child in this place if tha get upper hand of you all I dont sleep one nite cinc I herd this Horard nuse yull scuse my Bad Riting I peer Black man that wish you all wel and if it come to past will find you with all my mite But take that man live at Moncur office who call Him[self] Hart and Cry for the office the Head of the Black call Him Self Generall Wayne who kill all the Indians

this from your Dear well wisher

Poor Black Sam [7]

PART THREE

After Slavery

Norfolk Va 1864

Norfolk is a Dole place three years ago i was Dasant to say that i was free but thank God i can say so now the man i lived with is named W W hall he says that Woebelong to him in hell and he says that he wishes that yankees was at the Devel when i came a way i Diden no my a b c he had sould my brothers and sisters and would have sould me and mother and father if he coud for he had us paced upsen to richmond to sell he sead that the yankees had horns and thaer eyes was be hind them and thay had but one and thay us to [illegible] thay us to beat me this man was a negro byer he says before meny years he will be Doin the same bisniss he ses that the rebles will be her in may thank God that yankees come mond[ay] he was goin to send us to richmond the next monday that yankees come satday night, he carad my brother away he sad that youal black that you all had for legs like a hors and had one eye before and one behind and a horn on each side

—Emma Bolt

When i was liveing whith White People i was tide down hand and foot and they tide me to the Post and whip me till i Could not stand up and they tide my Close over my head and whip me much as they want and they took my Brother and sent him to Richmond to stay one year   And sent my Aunt my Sister my farther away too and said if he did not go away they would kill him   they said they was Goin to Put me in Prisens   But the light has come the Rebles is put down and Slavry is dead   God Bless the union Forever more   and they was puting people in tubs   and they stead me to Death and i hope slavly shall be no more   and they said that the yankees had horns and said that the yankees was Goin to kill us and somthing told me not to Believe them and somthing told me not to Be afraid   and when they Come hare they would not let me Come out to see them and when i was out in the Street they was Stead i would go away from them and they said I Better stay whith them for the yankees would kill me I would Better stay

—*Charlotte Ann Jackson,*
from H. L. Swint, ed.,
Dear Ones at Home (*1966*)

*S*ome blacks achieved freedom through self-purchase, cooperation with the American Colonization Society, escape, or open rebellion, but the society that "free blacks" confronted after slavery was far from equalitarian. Slavery existed in all of the Northern states until late in the eighteenth century, and in New York and New Jersey bondage was not fully eradicated until well into the nineteenth century. Even after emancipation in the North, an intense and pervasive racism remained, and oppression of the black population was the rule. Indeed, as the number of Northern free blacks increased, their status and rights tended to deteriorate. White fears of black economic, political, and sexual competition induced them to strip blacks of their rights as citizens, bar them from many jobs, and segregate them in inferior housing, in churches, and in almost all public accommodations. Most free Negroes lived in poverty, working in menial and service occupations which were threatened by competition from white immigrants. Moreover, from decade to decade, whites carried out racial violence against blacks; in the 1830's and 1840's, race riots occurred in Cincinnati, Philadelphia, and New York City. In 1863 white mobs killed scores of blacks in a New York City riot heightened by the tensions of the Civil War. A number of Northern states prohibited black emigration, and most states denied blacks the franchise. Less than 7 percent of the Northern black population, residing mainly in four New England states, was eligible to vote. In 1850 the fugitive slave laws, compelling all Northern citizens to cooperate in the capture and return of runaways to the South, were strengthened. And in 1857 the United States Supreme Court held in the Dred Scott case that blacks had never been and were not citizens. Blacks therefore could not claim the rights and privileges guaranteed to whites by the Constitution. In short, the 250,000 blacks living in the so-called free states were treated as inferior human beings and faced a precarious, even declining, existence. Not until the passage of the Thirteenth, Fourteenth, and Fifteenth Amendments to the Constitution after the Civil War did blacks gain the right to citizenship, the prospect of equal protection of the laws, and the possibility of voting.

Blacks who went North to Canada found their situation only slightly less discouraging, since Canada was host to racial discrimination. Before slavery was abolished in 1833, few white Canadians held slaves; government authorities sometimes even welcomed fugitive slaves and other black émigrés. By 1855, some 30,000 blacks were living in farming and commercial communities along the northern shore of Lake Ontario. As the number of blacks increased, however, so did white racism, and the threat remained that Canada might be annexed to the United States, where racism was rampant.

Blacks who emigrated to Liberia on the west coast of Africa fared little better than those who remained in the United States or Canada. Indeed the Liberian experience may have been even more disillusioning than the American one. Though nominally self-governing after 1847, the Liberians were unable to rejoin their ancestral families, states, or empires from which they had been previously enslaved. Nor were they able to escape the influence of the European imperial powers or of the United States itself. Developing a self-sufficient economy proved difficult, and conflicts with indigenous Africans were common. But at least the Liberian settlers had their own government and had fulfilled their dream of returning to their African homeland.

Despite escape and emigration, the reality of oppression remained for millions of American-born blacks living in the United States, Canada, and Africa. The Civil War came and slavery was abolished. The nation was "reconstructed" and the prospect of equality was raised. Yet emancipation came as a result of the necessities of war, and enfranchisement of blacks was intended to strengthen the Republican party. Neither measure reflected a moral commitment on the part of whites to full equality for blacks. Racism continued after the Civil War, and by the 1890's the gains of Reconstruction were dissipated.

CHAPTER SEVEN

The Fugitives

THE EXACT NUMBER of slaves who escaped successfully from the South will probably never be known, but at least 1,500 reached the free states or Canada each year before 1860. After arduous journeys through hundreds of miles of hostile territory, most of them finally settled into hard-working farm communities in northern Ohio, western New York, and Ontario, Canada. Other fugitives gravitated to the eastern cities of Philadelphia, New York, and Boston, where they worked mainly as day laborers and service tradesmen. Those who remained in the United States were not completely secure against professional kidnappers, slave catchers, and general harassment. Especially after 1850, when the fugitive slave law was strengthened, compelling Northern citizens to help in the capture of suspected runaways, many fugitives fled again to Canada or Africa.

The social backgrounds of the fugitives can also be approximately determined. The runaway advertisements, slave narratives, and interviews with Canadian émigrés—three reliable guides—reveal that most fugitives came from the Upper South, where escape was easiest, and many represented the better-educated slave elite. Skilled artisans, domestic servants, hirelings, and urban or industrial slaves formed a large proportion of the successful runaways. Indeed, by running away these slaves not only deprived Southerners of some of their most valuable

property but also contributed greatly to the emerging abolitionist movement in the North as well as to the development of their
own black communities.

    After escape from bondage, fugitives sometimes wrote
back to their old owners. Many of these letters were written
frankly as abolitionist propaganda. Frederick Douglass's letters
to Thomas Auld, like those of Henry Bibb to Silas Gatewood and
Daniel Laner, William Still to B. McKierson, and Jourdon Anderson to Colonel P. H. Anderson, are classics of a special genre
of antislavery literature. Other less famous fugitives—from
sheer bravado or in studied pain—also corresponded with their
old masters. These letters reveal much of the conditions of servitude, the reasons and methods of escape, and the hostility that
existed between masters and servants. Most masters were determined to repossess their lost property; for their part, fugitives
were proud of having absconded, expressed disdain for their
former owners, and regarded the future with optimism. Their
letters show glimpses of the quality of life for fugitives in the
North, the continuance of strong family and personal ties with
slaves still in the South, participation in religious activities and
the abolitionist movement, and political attitudes toward the
United States, Canada, and other countries.

                    St Catherines U C Nov 11 th 1840

Dear Sir,

    I now take this opportunity to inform you that I
am in a land of liberty, in good health. After I left
Winchester I staid in Pensylvania two years, & there
met some of your neighbors who lived in the house
opposite you, & they were very glad to see me; from
there I moved to this place where I arrived in the
month of August 1839.

I worked in Erie Penn where I met many of our neighbors from New Town. I there recieved 26 dollars a month.

Since I have been in the Queen's dominions I have been well contented, Yes well contented for sure, man is as God intended he should be. That is, all are born free & equal. This is a wholesome law, not like the Southern laws which puts man made in the image of God, on level with brutes. O, what will become of the people, & where will they stand in the day of Judgment. Would that the 5th verse of the 3d chapter of Malachi were written as with the pen of iron & the point of a diamond upon every oppressers heart that they might repent of this evil, & let the oppressed go free. I wish you might tell Addison John, & Elias to begin to serve the Lord in their youth, & be prepared for death, which they cannot escape, & if they are prepared all will be well, if not they must according to scripture be lost forever, & if we do not meet in this world I hope we shall meet in a better world where parting shall be no more.

And now I must here inform you that I was forced away in consequence of bad usage: only for that, & I should have been in America, though I do not regret coming, & if I had known how easy I could get along I should [have] started 10 years sooner, for it would have been better for me. Besides having a good garden, this summer I have raised 316 bushels potatoe, 120 bushels corn, 41 bushels buckwheat, a small crop of oats, 17 Hogs, 70 chickens.

I have paid 50 dolls rent this year: next year I expect to build. The Queen of England, has granted 50 acres of land, to every colored man who will accept of the gift, & become an actual settler. also a yoke of oxen, & plough for every two families. This a very great encouragement to those who have come here for the liberty which God had designed for them. Some have already gone, & others are going to take up the said land.

When I was coming to this place I stopped at Somerset, & worked there two weeks; there was an advertisement put up there for me, 200. dolls reward while I was there. I met James MacNear in Butler Co, Penn where I staid five months. I was in Pittsburg at the time that George Cremer was in pursuit of runaway servants. I was ostler for Isaac H Brittner in Cantanion 5 months, & in that time earned 60 dolls. I harvested while there cut 115 dozen a day & then went home & attended the stable, was counted the greatest cradler in Penn. There was no cradler known to cut that much in that part.

There was Chan Gatewood who expected to take me to the Rocky mountains, got sadly disappointed and lost his 700 dollars.

We have good schools, & all the colored population are supplied with schools. My boy Edward who will be six years next January, is now reading, & I intend keeping him at school until he becomes a good scholar.

I have enjoyed more pleasure in one month here than in all my life in the land of bondage. And now you may believe me though unwelcome as the news may be, but it is true Joseph Taper has a commission from Col Clarck of this place, & is Capt of 40 men.

After you read this I shall be very gratified to you if you will send this to Bryan Martin Stevens. I send my respects to Mrs Stevens. I thank her for her kind usage to me in time of sickness. She acted more like a mother than a mistress. Respects to all who know me. I hope this letter will find them all well & as for old Milla, I expect she is dead, & gone to the devil long ago, if she is not, I think the imps are close at her heels, & will soon put her where there are nothing else but *nasty, stinking black dogs* a plenty.

My wife and self are sitting by a good comfortable fire happy, knowing that there are none to molest or make afraid. God save Queen Victoria. The Lord bless her in this life, & crown her with glory in the world to come is my prayer, Yours with much respect

most Obt, Joseph Taper [1]

Canaday   No 1 1850

Mr. John Walker request from Mr Rightso   He is in canaday and wantes me to Right to you For him   he stat in his letter that he is well And hop that thes few lines may find you All the sam   he wantes you to tell his farther That he is duing very well so far and

[153]

he   He wantes to hear from his wife and he Wantes
to buy her and all the children and if you or anney
boday wantes to Right to him   They can direct thar
letter to Mrss ann eliza diges As was but her nam is
ann eliz James know

John it is your cusen ann J. Walker and if you wantes
to hear from brother Thomas Rirghtso you may
wright to me   I live in boston Mass en south russel
street nomber 31 and thar you May find me   and he
wantes you to Right Him as soon as git this letter and
let him hear From you and all the frindes that wantes
to hear from him   you tell them wher to Rite   And
Clous the letter yours Respetfuly

                              Mrss Ann Eliza James [2]

Dear sir I am saft and got their Saft and man [?] that
month $2 000000 [?] I am permited to go to thar
houus and dine with them

                              Canaday December the 5 1850

My Dear Mr John Walker

Dear Sir you hav afforded to me murch Plurcher in
ancing my letter and dear sir your Letter I recive it on
the 28 and was glad to hear that you and all is will and
I wish you to tell All that wantes to know how I made
my ascape that I made it in the knight when the Moon
was gon away and thar was no eyes To see but god
and it was threw him that I made my ascape and it is
threw him that I am know gitting along and ples to
say to my Farther and to my fartherinlaw that I

feel happy in my ascape untill I thinkes about my
Wife and I hope that you bouth will talk to her and
tell Her to be not dischomfierd for I thinks that I shall
see you agin   Tell him to tell her if she is not sole at
Chrismous she mus let me know how she and the
childrens are agatthing along   And dear farther ples
to see her and see If thar is anney way for me to Send
a man to by her and tell her that if anney man comes
to her And tell her that he wantes to by her Tell to ask
him wher he live and if he say that [he] liv in england
and He tell you he do you ask him if he know Mr
Rightso and if he say no you May not go with him but
and if he say that he do you may com.

    all I wantes is En oppotunity to send a man to by
her for thear is men that wood com on And by her at
a wurd   thell them that the pepol is sendding up
thar cryes For all that is know in bondiges I don know
no man by ailler [?] her thay Are all plesent and cam

    and all so I will cloes My letter By asking you all
to pray and if thar is anney that wantes to Com tell
them to com on for thar is Room a nof for us all.

                                    yours respectfully
                                    Mr Thomas Rightso [3]

Cusen John Walker my lov to you Sir and when you
writ me a gain you ples to send you lov to ann Eliza
James

And hear is for sur [———?] and meney other that I
could tell you. Giv my lov to peter clepchip the bot-
tem binder and to as meney as you will and tell them

that her is Room her For them You may Right me as mouch as you Ples and let me hear From you

Mr Thomas Rightso [4]

Other fugitives tried to communicate with their friends and family still in bondage, suggesting the strong personal and religious ties between fugitives and their friends. One of the more interesting letters that has survived is by William Thompson, the slave fireman in the engine room of the Andrew Brown Lumber Company of Natchez, Mississippi, written to James Mathews, a head raftsman (previously mentioned in Part I) responsible for rafting lumber to the company sawmill. In 1854, Thompson had tried to escape but was soon captured. Thompson's successful escape a year later was facilitated by his ability to forge a pass with which he made his way to freedom. Rumors that he had been seen in New Orleans or on steamboats continued to circulate until Thompson sent a letter from Canada back to his friends.

London [Canada]
May 14, 1855

James Mathews, Sir,

I take up my Pen most Respectfully for to write to you hoping that this will find you and your family in good health as this leaves me in at Present, thanks be to God [for] all His Mercies to me. Sir, sience I have left Employ I have been on the Great Western Railroad driving an Engine. I give my best Respects to Mrs. Marton and family, Andrew Bron and family, and all my Enqiren friends. Sir, I now state to you the Reates of this Country. This is a good Wheat country, and Oats and everything in proportion, unless Corn, and you can beat this Country growing Corn. Wheat is 2 dollars pr bushel, Oats 4 shilling pr bushell, Pork 4 dollars pr 100 lbs. Butter is 20 ct. pr lbs. and everything else is dear in proportion.

When you write direct your letter to E. M. Jones, New Lon[don], Canada, West, for William Thompson.

No more at present, But I Remain your true friend

William Thompson [5]

When you write let me know if you got anny word from my Mother since i lift there.

CHAPTER EIGHT

Back to Africa

SLAVES STRUGGLED TO return to their African homeland from the moment they were forced to leave African
shores. Mutinies broke out on board slave-trading ships, and
once in the New World blacks began to organize to go back to
Africa. Though most black Americans seemed hostile or at best
apathetic about emigration, a few free blacks in the Northern
and border states were greatly interested. As early as 1816, Paul
Cuffee, a black merchant and shipbuilder, transplanted thirty-
eight Negroes to the British colony of Sierra Leone. The deterioration of the free black's status in the 1840's and 1850's increased immigration even among integrationists like Frederick
Douglass. In 1859 and 1860, Martin Delany, a Harvard-trained
physician, led an expedition to the Niger River valley to explore
the feasibility of resettlement. Even after the Civil War brought
legal freedom and attempts at racial reconstruction awakened
hopes of ultimate integration into American life, the idea of returning to Africa was kept alive by Bishop Henry M. Turner
and, later, by Marcus Garvey.

While some blacks attempted to migrate to Africa to escape
oppression, whites sought to rid the United States of troublesome blacks. Thomas Jefferson and Abraham Lincoln, as well as
other leading Americans, devised schemes to deport blacks—
especially slave rebels and the despised free Negroes. The most

determined white organization was the American Colonization Society, founded January 1, 1817, by leading politicians and ministers. Among the men who supported the American Colonization Society were John Marshall, Henry Clay, Francis Scott Key, and Richard Rush. Like most white Americans, the colonizationists believed that cultural inferiority prohibited blacks' incorporation into the American republic and that the only viable solution to the race problem was to ship them back to Africa. Besides, Liberia, the colonizationist-established enclave on the west coast of Africa, would serve as a foothold where white missionaries could convert African peoples to Christianity and white businessmen could sell black people American goods.

The desire of whites to pack blacks off to Africa cooled most free blacks on emigration. In fact, the vast majority of the free black population vigorously opposed colonization and the ACS. About half of the Liberian settlers were slaves manumitted on the condition that they leave the country; but some slaves believed that by working through the ACS they might obtain their freedom and, then, somehow remain in the land of their birth. Still other blacks saw Liberia as a refuge from misery in the United States, and sincerely regarded the colony as their homeland.

The letters written by slaves to the American Colonization Society reveal the problems encountered by blacks seeking to reach Africa: lack of money, legal obstacles, dishonest lawyers, and deceitful owners. More significant is the intensely religious, nationalistic identification with Africa. Many of these letters were published in 1927 by the pioneer black historian, Carter Woodson, in *Mind of the Negro*. Printed here are several letters which have not been previously published.

Atlanta Geo   March 13 th 1855

Dear friend   I understood your name was Mitchel which I will now say to you that we are inclined to go to Liberia & is left free by Mr F Gideons & it is impos-

sible for us to get thare with out Essistance   we understand you are the person that is appointed to attend to the free negroes that is left in this way. Dear
sir we do hope you will be so kind as to assist us in
some way   thare is a number of us that is all left free
say thare is 19 left in this way   please to write me
. . . [————?] & please to direct your letter to Eliza-
beth Halebook to the city of Atlanta fulton county
Gea   we are on the Record free in this place   please
to write in haste as we are in such distress   you will
here in haste from good white people hour master
left 100 hundred dollars to pay hour Expen-
ses   apiece there stan 100 a piece for us to live on til
we could get a start   please if we have a mistake in
your name of being a manager to take charg of such
business as ours we hope you will write imeadiateley
then you shall have all particulars   we End with
subscribing hour selves your

> humble Servants
> Eav Gideons
> Samuel Gideons [1]

> Lynchburg   Septr 6th 1855

Dear Sir

I take the liberty to write you a few lines by the
advice of Mrs Wm Blackford to make some enquiries
concerning emigration from here to Liberia this Fall.

I wish to know if I can obtain a passage on the
packet that will sail (in November I think) to Liberia.

And if I can will you be so good as to let me know as soon as possible as I want to get ready. And I do not wish to stay any longer in America.

I want to know exactly whether if I go at the expense of the State of Virginia, I shall be able to return when I please, as I shall probably wish to return to bring my wife and children. My Misstress died the 1st day of last Decr and left me free to go to Liberia. She lived at Dr Leyburn's near Lexington, her name Miss Sally Price. The provisions of the will were that if I did not leave the country in a year I was to be sold. I have a wife and four children. I have not been able to get these as they belong to a lady here, but hope to return for them.

Dear Sir I wish you to sympathize with me here, you know that of course nature binds and undoubtedly I must love a dear wife and children, but as circumstances are such that we are to be separated I will trust my master for the future to assist me in the attempt, knowing that He has said—"that all things work together for good to them that love God." And I know that His word is sure and that His promise stands fast. Others have tried before me and have found that they have come out conquerers over many such trials.

My wife is so good and valuable to her owners that it makes them unwilling to part with her, but God has the hearts of all men in His keeping, and I am willing to trust Him for all.

There were seven liberated beside myself by this lady. One of my brothers will go with me. We will let you hear from us all as soon as we hear from you.

Please direct your letter to me, to Mrs Mary B. Blackford, Lynchburg Va

Your humble Servant
Wm James Henry [2]

Charleston   Dec 23rd 1855

Revd & Dear Sir—I would be exceedingly glad if you could do me the kindness by sending me the Skethes of Liberia by Dr. Lugenbeel—& the information about going to Liberia as I am an old friend of Liberia—I should like to hear all that I can about her—for I believe that Africa is the land of promise & rest to the Colored man a land of pure liberty & freedome. I only would to God that I could go there—but it is out of my power so to do—But O Lord Our God hasten the day when every Color'd Soul in America—or in any other part of the world may return to Africa—a land of rest—a land of peace—a land of happiness—a land [of] glory—a land of exceeding great Joy—which Thee Lord our God has given to the Sons of Ham as an inheritance for ever—do send them as soon as Convenient & direct to my name—Charleston post office & oblige your humble servant

M. G. Camplin— [3]

Richmond Va   April 24 th 1856

Rev. W. McLain

Dear Sir you say in the 1st No of the African Repository of the present year that you had in per-sisinon   A No of the Skeaches on Africa which you would send to any whom would write for them   you will do me the greates favor by sending me those Skeaches as it is [my] intantion to go to africa   I shall be glad to get all information of it I can for I feel that I may do some good there prehaps as I can read & write slitly   I am now be longing to mr Jas K Lee of this City whom bot me for perpose of perchesing myslef for to go to africa & should it please the almighty god to enable me to get [free] I plege myslef to do all that I [can] for the good of that Country & its people   Direct yours to Jas. K. Lee atty at law Richmond Va

I Remain your obedent Servt
James Benjimond Burrell [4]

Richmond Va   May 12 th 1856

Rev Wm McLain   Secy of the Colonization Society

Dr Sir   it [is]with great pleasure that I am seated this evening for the object of writing you a few lines as I have seen the account of you furnishing coppys [of] Lugenbeel & copies about going to Liberia   I shall be very glad to get bouth of those copies for I am trying to mak up the Some .of money to finsh paying for

[164]

myslef so as to go to liberia ware I trust god that I may
doe some good if it should please god to spare me to
get there

Send yours to care of Lee & Bayly

> I Am your most umble Servant
> James B Burrell [5]

CHAPTER
NINE

Letters from Liberians

WITHIN FOUR YEARS of its founding in 1817, the American Colonization Society had obtained from local African leaders a stretch of coastal land near the Mesurado River. The first permanent settlers arrived in 1822, the colony was called Liberia, and its capitol, Monrovia, was named after U.S. President James Monroe, a slave-owner. By 1867 the ACS had transported to Africa about 12,000 American blacks, whose social backgrounds have yet to be fully explored. Of the African immigrants, 4,541 had been born free in the United States, 5,957 had been emancipated by masters on the condition that they go to Africa, 753 had been manumitted for other reasons, and 1,227 (whose backgrounds are not known) were settled by the Maryland Colonization Society at "Maryland in Liberia" near Cape Palmas. In addition, 5,722 Africans captured from slave-traders were sent by the U.S. Navy to Liberia under the custodianship of the ACS, which received congressional grants for the purpose.

For the first twenty-five years, the pioneer emigrants were a heterogeneous group. Coming from all areas of the South as well as from the free states, they were fairly evenly divided between men, women, and children. One in four of those over ten years old was literate, which compared favorably with the 5 percent literacy rate among American slaves. Some had been artisans or house servants; most were farm hands with few skills and little property. Virtually all were entirely dependent on the American Colonization Society and their former masters for supplies and money for their first months or years in Liberia.

The early settlers faced many problems and disappointments. Acclimatization to the new environment took an extremely heavy toll, and morbidity and mortality rates were tragically high compared with other emigration and settlement movements. Of 4,454 arrivals between 1820 and 1843, for example, 2,198 died and only 645 Liberian-born children survived. Economic instability and diplomatic conflicts continued to plague the colonists until the 1860's. England, France, and Spain were hostile, and the Liberians had great difficulty suppressing the illegal slave trade conducted from various "factories" along the coast at Cape Mount, north of Monrovia, and especially at Trade Town, below the capitol at Bassa. Not until after 1842 did the U.S. government take action against the trade; finally, in 1846 and 1849, determined attacks were launched against the slave traders with some cooperation from the British. Equally as serious were the wars between the Liberians and the African "natives." Conflicts with the Des and Golas were especially pronounced in 1822 and 1832, with the Krus and Golas from 1838 to 1840, with the Bassas in 1851, with the Krus from 1850 to 1860, and with the Grebos in 1856–1857.

The Liberians were under the control of the white governors of the American Colonization Society until 1846, when the society resolved that "the time has arrived when it is expedient for the people of the Commonwealth of Liberia to take into their own hands the sole work of self-government. . . ." Consequently, on July 26, 1847, the Liberians issued their Declaration of Independence which detailed how blacks were oppressed in the United States and looked "with anxiety for some asylum from deep degradation . . . and the most grinding oppression." "American benevolence and philanthropy" had selected Africa "for our future home," stated the Liberians, who hoped to "enjoy those rights and privileges and exercise and improve those faculties which the God of nature has given to us in common with the rest of mankind." The Liberians established a republican form of government, modeled their flag on that of the United States, and appealed to the "nations of Christendom" to regard them with "sympathy and friendly considerations." In 1848 and 1849 the European powers (as well as the Republic of Haiti) recognized Liberian independence; but the United States withheld recognition until 1862 (as it did with Haiti), in order not to receive a black ambassador in Washington. The American Colonization Society nevertheless continued to sponsor settlers until the 1890's.

The first four Liberian presidents were mulattos, including Joseph Jenkins Roberts, 1848–1855, and Stephen Allen Benson, 1856–1863. The Liberian ruling elite generally came from the lighter-skinned group favored by American masters. These Liberians had a patronizing—if not hostile—attitude toward the indigenous Africans, and most Liberians believed it was their Christian mission to "civilize" their African brothers. Christian churches, schools, and literary societies were established, and efforts were made to instill Western culture in the African population.

From Liberia, ex-slaves wrote to their families and their former masters in America. These letters reveal the Liberians' reasons for emigrating, the hardships and disillusionment facing settlers, the strong ties among slave families, loneliness for black friends and relatives, attitudes toward former owners and the United States, feelings toward indigenous Africans, and, most interestingly, the intense identification of American blacks with their African homeland.

Among the more devout colonizers was John Hartwell Cocke of Virginia, a tobacco estate owner who had served as a general in the War of 1812. Forsaking a political career, Cocke was noted for his reforming interests in scientific agriculture, education, transportation improvements, and the temperance and antitobacco movements. He became president of the American Temperance Union in 1836, and gave up planting tobacco after 1839, choosing to raise grains and cotton instead.

Although he was a large slave-owner, Cocke regarded

slavery as a great curse, and was known throughout Virginia for his opposition to bondage. After much consideration, however, he came to believe that emancipation would have to be accomplished "by a process so slow as to preclude the men of any one generation from the honor of its accomplishment." Most Virginians, he judged, would acquiesce in a plan of freedom only if they were compensated at a fair price for the loss of their property, and only if the freedmen were removed from the country. Thereafter for many years Cocke served as vice-president of the American Colonization Society, which favored gradual emancipation and urged the deportation of free blacks to Africa.

Cocke held that before the slaves could be freed and deported they should be educated, trained, and "civilized." In 1852 he confided to his diary his belief that Virginia slaves in the hands of humane masters could not be freed to their advantage in their "ignorant and debased" condition. In addition, he considered it his duty to hold his slaves for their own good. And, as he judged, because their bondage had made them unfit for liberty, "the obligation of preparing them for freedom and bestowing it upon them when so prepared" was his. To prepare his slaves for freedom, Cocke established an experimental plantation in Alabama—named, appropriately, Hopewell—where he encouraged the religious and moral instruction of the slaves he intended to return to Africa. In 1833 he freed one slave family and sent its members to Liberia, and in later years he and his neighbors sent other slaves to Africa. In 1843 he wrote confidentially to John McDonogh that he had for several years been engaged in a secret colonization plan which would "probably require some 5 or 6 years to accomplish."

By 1856, however, Cocke had become disappointed with the intellectual and moral improvement of his Hopewell slaves, who had failed "to bring their minds up to the conception of the dignity of Liberty." In his will in 1859, Cocke therefore bequeathed his slaves to his grandsons rather than manumitting them. Only Lucy Skipwith, the plantation school mistress, was to be freed and sent to Africa with her family. But when Union troops brought freedom to Alabama, she rejected the offer.

One of the most important American colonizers who sent slaves to Liberia was John McDonogh of Louisiana. A poor youth, McDonogh moved from Maryland to Louisiana in 1800; within forty years he had acquired several plantations and a large brickyard worked by approximately 200 slaves. He was one of the Crescent City's leading merchants, with a reputation for eccentricity. Beginning in 1822, McDonogh permitted his slaves to work for themselves half of each Saturday, while keeping the Sundays "holy" with regular attendance and preaching in church. He paid his men 62½ cents per day in the summer and 50 cents per day in the winter; the women and younger slaves received lesser amounts. In 1825 McDonogh instituted a plan of emancipation whereby if the slaves worked several *extra* hours in the mornings and evenings, they might, after fifteen years of good behavior, accumulate enough credit to purchase themselves and their children. According to McDonogh's recollection, all the slaves present at the announcement of this plan "lent an attentive ear; and again, with eyes streaming with tears, assured me of their full determination to devote their days and nights for the honor of God, the happiness of their children, and the carrying out of the plan I had devised for their benefit." McDonogh noticed that after the plan was agreed upon, "an entire change appeared to come over them; they were no longer apparently the same people; a sedateness, a care, an economy, and industry took possession of them. . . . They became temperate, moral, religious." McDonogh claimed that he treated his blacks well, used only black "commanders" as overseers, permitted them to cultivate garden plots, gave out Christmas presents, emphasized religious training, and staged trials with black juries. But he also threatened them with sale for misconduct, and at least two slaves were jailed and sold.

After 1830, McDonogh actively participated in and regularly contributed to the American Colonization Society, and upon his death in 1850 he bequeathed to the organization a forty-year annuity of up to $25,000 per year. Finally, on June 11, 1842, more than eighty of McDonogh's slaves sailed for Liberia, and a month later the master proudly explained and recommended to others his self-purchase and colonization plans in a long, patronizing, and widely reprinted open letter to the *New Orleans Commercial Bulletin*. In his private correspondence, however, McDonogh revealed his true motives governing his colonization efforts. "I have often reflected," McDonogh confided to a sympathetic Virginia planter, "asking wisdom from the source of all Wisdom to direct me for the separation of the two races of men . . . knowing that each and every one of them, sent from this country to their fatherland, prepared with the love of God, in their hearts, will become a humble instrument in his hand for the bringing of the heathen to him, and that such was the plan in infinite wisdom in permitting them to be brought into slavery [so that] their descendents might acquire among us the knowledge of him and in good time return with the pearl of inestimable value to them in that dark land and proclaim his glorious name. . . . My own opinion is that without separation of the races, extermination of one or the other must inevitably take place. The two races can never inhabit together in a state of equality in the same country. They may for a short time live together in the capacity of Master and slave, but as equals and Brethren never—"

When McDonogh's freedmen reached Africa, they began to correspond with their former owner. Significantly, most of the freedmen addressed McDonogh as "Father," "Parent," and "Beloved Benefactor." They still regarded themselves as McDonogh's "faithful servant," and "affectionate son," even retaining their master's last name. Such accommodating attitudes may have been insincere or a means of obtaining further material assistance from the United States; but they do suggest the extent of the master's impact on his former slaves.

Monrovia, Nov. 17th, 1845
Liberia – Wt.

Mr. Jno. McDonogh,
Dear Beloved Benefactor,

This is the first oppor. that I have had to send a communication since my arrival here. Therefore I do embrace in hoping that this may meet you in good health. Mr. and Mrs. Gullen are well and are doing very well at present and we are all quite sorry that others have not done according to the promise they made when we was about to take our departure from you in regard to the part they were destined to go to which was Sinoe, but we do beg of you to overlook our wrongs in this matter, as it was owing to the Governor and many other persons here that we did not go further for they informed us particularly that the condition of the place at the time was such that we had better remain here—for the population was 50 scanty there, and the Country people being much more uncivilized than they were here that during our sickness in the fever we would be robbed of what few articles we had. But since I had the pleasure of receiving such an important and animating correspondence from you, speaking of this matter, the Generality of us are now resolved to go there though I have commenced forming here and have a considerable tract of land under cultivation.

Your letters arrived here in the latter part of September. But I am sorry to inform you that the articles you sent us we did not get. Some of them for the Barque renown, however, reached our port, but the vessel that brought the letters always brings us the intelegence that was a stove on a rock near an island I suppose 200 miles or more to the westward of us and it was much difficulty that they succeeded in saving all the Emigrants, but their cargo was all lost—Now Beloved Father we do earnestly request of you not forsake us for our delinquency in not being as vigilant as you thought we might have been. But we do intend to mend our pace and act consistent with your will— since we came to this country and got rid of the fever, we like the country very well and our only grievance now is for us to get to Sinoe which we have been prevented from emigranting to since we have got well on account of our shortage of many to defray our Expense. But they are trying to do all they can now toward getting there. Please remember my respects to George Remy and Noel Ruffile and my best wishes and respects to Fanny Grinos and my dear Aunt May. And Remember my respects and sincere wishes to all inquiring friends and tell all to Remember us in their prayers for it is much needed in our land. But as paper is very scarce with us here and the Barque in our port is about to leave I must come to a close Giving you all the thanks for your Unspeakable kindness and Goodness towards us which by me shall never be forgotten. Amelia Gray is dead and Sally Hines and Dabney and Peter Young, Maria Kelley and Lucy Kelley—Rendall Brige.

But I bid you all adieu, and I do remain,

Yours most sincere and affectionate
and Beloved Son Until Death
James M. George [1]

Sottra Kross,
Dec. 28th, 1845

Dear Father—

I have a great reason to and thank God that I am
yet spared to see the close of another year, and I hope
that by his blessing these will find you and all inquiring friends the same. I am at this time with the Mission at Sottra Kros and we are all well at present. I
suppose you heard of Mrs. Connelly's visit to the
states. She reached here on the fifteenth of October
last. She has been confined since that and has a fine
daughter. On her return to this country she brought
out a young woman of color with her as my assistant
and teacher. But alast she is not, for she has been
called home to rest. She lived little over one month
after her arrival here, but we have every reason to
believe that her end was peace. This is the third death
we have had in this Mission this year. In the first place
we lost a boy with the consumption. The next one
died very sudden. He was taken sick about ten o'clock
in the evening with a pain in the stomach. We gave
him medicine but all for no purpose for he died in
about two hours after he was taken. The first boy
went home when he was taken very sick to his father
and died in house but the second boy died in the Mission yard which caused a great many of the scholars
to run off, so our school is quite small at this time.
The people among whom we live are very ignorant
and superstituous if any one died they will say that
someone has bewitched and very often will go off to
the gran devil man as he is sometimes called and got
him to tell who, it was that bewitched the person that

[175]

died, and if he choose to tell them a lie on any person, they catch the person and give him what they call sassa wood. This sassa wood is the bark of a tree that grows in the swamps. There are two kinds—one kind is very poisonous—if the person that is accused has a plenty of money the will give him the worst kind for the sake of getting his money. If he will pay them e good some they will give him the weak kind, but a poor person will be sure to come off badly, but they did not give it for either of the young men that died in the Mission.

Now, dear Father, I hope you will answer this by the first chance, and hope that by the blessing of God you will be spared not only to answer this one but a great many more.

Your humble servant
W. W. McDonogh [2]

P.S. I have not seen my mother for one year and half—the last time I heard from her they were all well.

Monrovia, Liberia
August 7, 1846

My dear Master and friend, Mr. McDonogh—

I take up my pen to write you a few lines, hoping they will find you in the same good health I write them, and that you will live a long number of years blessed by the Lord in every way, and to do more and more good on earth.

Oh sir, your kind letter to me of January 2 is received and I read it with tears of joy to think you write to one so low as me and call me your dear son. I read it to all your people here and it made us all rejoice, and our tears to flow, when we remembered you and all your kindness, and we should never see you any more in this World, but we trust we are only separated for a short time to meet again, to part no more.

You ask me to tell you all about this country, if it is a good country, and what we raise. I will tell you Sir, as well as I can. It is a fine country, the land is rich and produces everything but wheat—all kinds of Garden stuff as in America—cabbage, Pease, Beans, Concumbers, Melons, Onions, Tomatoes, Rice, Indian Corn, Cassada, fruits of all kinds, Oranges, &c. &c.

The country is healthy for the Black people and our children is increasing in numbers. We are all happy and contented, as we can be, seeing that we are separated from you, our Dear friend and father, and we would not change this country for any other part of the World. We have plenty of everything but clothing which is very dear. All our people send their love to you, and all our friends with you, and tell you that their prayers are constantly put up to the throne of Grace, night and day, for blessings on your heads, I am in haste to write this as the vessel that carries out sails to-day, but will write you Dear Father, again soon.

Oh, my prayer to God is that he will bless and preserve you long in life, and at death receive you into heaven.

All from your faithful servant and son,
John Aiken [3]

Oct. 7th 1846 King Wil's Town

Dear Father,

I have again taken up my pen to address you a few lines hoping that these will find you in as good health as they leaves me at this.

I thank my God that he has still given me in health and strength at this time to address you. We are all well at this time, that is the Mission family, Mr. and Mrs. Conolly, Mr. & Mrs. Priest.

Mrs. Conolly you recollect was in America last year. After his return to this country she was delivered of a fine daughter but alast the Lord has seen proper to take it to himself.

Mrs. Priest had a fine son and he has been taken also. They could not have been taken in a better time for they were both infants.

Thee Lord givest and Thee Lord taketh. Blessed be the name of the Lord. I paid a visit to my mother and Family the first of this year and found them in good health. I spent two months and a half with them during which time I assisted my Brother in clearing and planting a fine crop of rice, corn and capedars. He has at this time on his farm about twenty-four or five bound boys, some of them ware taken from on board of a slaver by an American Man of War. I think he has now about sixty acres of land under cultivation or very near it. My visit was in January. February and a part of March. I then returned to my labor among the hethen.

Dear Father,

I have just been reading again your very kind letter to me just before I left College. I do assure you Sir that there is nothing on earth that gives me more pleasure than it does to think that I have such a friend and adviser as you are for no one but a father can give to a son such advice, surely not, and the more I read it the more I am encouraged to press forward in my calling as a teacher, and may the Lord give me grace to run and not be weary for without him we are nothing and can do nothing. I praise his holy name that my lot was not case in a heathen country and among heathen parents but in a Christian Country and among Christian parents and friends and that too in the hands of one who has been a father unto me instead of a cruel possessor. When I was young and foolish you took me among from my father and mother into your own dwelling and brought me up as a Son instead of a servant. I ofton thought hard of it at the time but now I find it was for my own benefit and not yours that you took so much paine in bringing me up in the ways of truth and honesty for I find now that truth and honesty is the best capitals that a man can possess in this world. It is true that wealth makes many friends but their friendship is but deceit. An honest man is said to be the noblest work of his creator. Had I been permitted to run about as many of my age, were, I should have today been as ignorant as they are. But thanks to my Creator I was not. And to you dear Father words cannot express my gratitude to you for your care towards me during my younger days for youth is truly the time to lay up for old age. And I hope that I have commenced on a good foundation for you have given me precept upon precept and line upon line and may the Lord give me grace to keep them all the days of my life. And now dear father permit me to give you an imperfect statement of the productions of the Country and then close for the night. The first and greatest is *Rice, Sweet potatoes, Lima beans, okra, pease, radish, cabbage, Parsnaps, Cucumbers, Greens, Casadavas,* or *Casavas, Yams, Corn, Collards, Cymblain, Arrowroot, Carrots* a few, the *Paupew* which grows on a tree, *Pumpkins, Parsley, Mustard—water-melon, Mus-melon, Mango, Plums, orange. Rose apples, Sour top, Guava, Camorind, Plantains, Banana, Gramevua, Dill, Limes* and *Lemons.*

Domesticated

Cows, Bullocks, Swine, Sheep, Goats, Ducks, Fowls, pidgeons, turkeys very few.

I will not attempt to give you a list of the wild animals, and the different kinds of fish that we have here at this time, should you wish to know I will give it to you at some future time should my life be spared.

I should like very much dear father to see you once more before we leave this world for it would be a source of great delight to me. But I will never consent to leave this country for all the pleasures of America combined together to live, for this is the only place a colored person can enjoy his liberty for there exists no prejudice of color in this country but every man is free and equal.

Please to remember me to all our friends and acquaintances, to Mr. Durnford and Son, and Uncle James Thornton and Par Houvel, and all the rest.

And now my Dear Father, I close this letter hoping that you will let me hear from you soon.

And may the Lord who is able to do all things, protect and deliver from all dangers seen and unseen and grant you strength for many days and years yet to come, is the prayer of your humble servant.

W. W. McDonogh [4]

The Hon. Walter mention in his last letter to me that he had bought me a watch with the money that you sent him for me.

Please to let me know what has become of David.

Monrovia Liberia March 25th 1849

My Dear Father,

Your kind and cheering letter bearing date January 8th 1847 came safe to hand on the 14 of present month. I cannot express to you the joy it afforded me also my Mother and Sister, Mr. Ellis I have found out to be a fine man and I hope good Christian he preached yesterday it being the Sabbath I also ment to hear him and am much pleased with him we are all well Mr. Ellis is at my house and has been to see me several times.

My Dear Father I have wrote you by every chance but have not received letters from you as I expected but as I wrote you in my last hope you will do that is to write and direct your letters to me but to the care of Walter Lowrie of New York and he of course will forward them to me as I am now acting agent for the Mission at Sottra Kroo, I have been very much disappointed in not receiving letters from you by the way of New York as you promised to communicate with me that way.

I have received no letters but by vessels direct from New Orleans since I have been here, the letters of Andrew Dumford has been wrote better than two years ago and if you had have sent it on to New York I should have received long since I have also wrote you to send me something and I wrote to you as a son to a father as I have no one on earth that can render me the assistance that you can, I again repeat the request you stated in your letter that you did not know of the vessel sailing until about an hour before she sailed I was surprized to hear it but I believe if you had have known it you would have sent me something if it was only a yarn of cloth so I hope as I am told this vessel will be acceptable whether any goods or provisions. I know that you cant send anything but by the vessel direct from New Orleans and I certainly look for something by the first vessel from there as the amount of three or five hundred dollars would be of no consequence to a man of your wealth and as I find myself so much in need in this hard country and seeing and believing you know the same is my reason for making this request of you. I wrote you sometime since concerning Gray's Property in Gretna the children as I stated them are in my hands and I find it difficult to support them and school them both, so I beg of you to have the property sold and send the amount out to me for the children in anything you think suitable, I was in hopes that it would have been before this time.

My Dear Father I must inform you that I am married and living as comfortable as can be expected, our people are doing tolerably well they saw timber planks and shingles and make farms. Cornelius is dead the rest are all well. My Dear Father I remember the good counsel you gave me so often and pray that the Lord may bless protect and defend you through life by his un erring counsel and that when the voyage of life is over and he has no more for you to do on earth he will take you to live with him in glory.

I did as you told me with Washington's letters and as an opportunity afford on the sixteenth of this month I sent it to him. I got a letter from him about three weeks ago he was then well. Mother and Julia sends a thousand loves to you and prays to be remembered by you at a throne of grace. By this vessel would have come to New Orleans on a visit but I could not bring my business to a close sufficient to leave and I wish you Dear Father to write me whether there will be any difficulty and how the law is touching persons returning to visit. I have between thirty and forty acres of my farm under cultivation I have Cassadoes Potatoes Arrowroot Ginger Ground nuts Pepper Bushes with number Orango trees Mango Paw Paw Pine Apple Guava Sugarcane Lime trees and my dwelling on my farm is enclosed by a lime heage I have between three and four hundred Coffee trees which I planted from the seed in a nursery and I grew them and let them out and they are now bearing from half pounds to a pound each, I have also Cocoa Nut Trees I have sent you a specimen of the Coffee from my farm.

Mother has done pretty well with Turkeys from those five she brought out she can show twenty or thirty besides what she has made use of, she has some of the old ones also, this Coffee I send just as a curiosity and to show that I took your advice in farming I have seen a man from New Orleans that I knew while ther and he told me that our Old George Martin was dead also Mr. Pollock the Notary as well as many others that I asked him about. My Dear Father I wish to enquire of our old friend John Hudson I hope he is well give my best respects to him if he is yet alive. I am very thankful to you for those newspapers you were kind enough to send me I hope you will send them to me by every chance I have sent you a few of ours, I hope Dear Father that you will send me also a few working tools such as axes spades and the like as they are very hard to get here and very useful.

Dear Father I have sent some letters in your package for different persons which I hope you will give them for me. Madam Egretto lives just back of your house and now dear Father I must bring my letter to a close I hope to hear from you in short.

> I remain dear Father
> Your affectionate son
> G. R. Ellis McDonogh [5]

> Sottra Kroo,
> March 7th 1848

Mon. Sir:

I have taken this opportunity of addressing you a few lines to inform you that I am still in the land of the living and enjoying the rights of man for although I am in a land of darkness I have nothing to fear—my wants are few and of course easily supplyed—not like you who are living in a land of milk and honey and yet never satisfied.

I have lived in the same land myself and had the pleasure of enjoying all that the heart could wish for or that would make one happy and yet I was not willing to denie myself of the lease thing, but, alas, what a change has since taken place. Things that seemed to have been of so much value to me in those times are no more to me now than idle dreams when compared with my present views of them, all that I now wish for is just enough to make me confortable and happy while I live in this world for we are told in scripture that we can carry nothing out of it when we go hence; and now, Dear Sir, I think I have found one that is able and willing to help me on in my labors as a Missionary among the heathen. She is a young lady from the West—she was expected out with the Rev. Mr. Ellis by whom you wrote me a year ago; she came out last year say in October and has gone through her acclimating fevers very well and is now prepared for the business of a mission being brought up and educated in one of the best Christian familys in Cincinnati. You may know that she is worthy of your dear Washington. She was brought up in the family of the Rev. Mr. Biggs of the above named place. I expect to marry her in a short time if life last perhaps before this reaches you. I hope that you will be so kind as to send me out something to start on in the way of making a liveing or to live on for you know that my time is all spent in the Lords' service and not in worldly gains or speculations.

Please inform me when you write me when you heard from David last and what is his occupation.

Now, dear parent, I will close by wishing you long life and happiness, with my best wishes to you and all my friends.

Your obt. Servant
Washington W. McDonogh. [6]

St Pauls River New Orleans, Liberia
October 24th 1849.

Mr. John McDonough,

Dear Sir,

Having an opportunity of forwarding letters to
the United States by the Liberia Packet which will sail
in a few days I embrace this good opportunity of writing you by her.

This Sir I am happy to say leave in the en-
joyment of good health also my family and wishing
these times may find you and yours enjoying the same
blessing. Since we have heard from you we have had
some deaths out of our member. They are Mr. James
Fullor, Alexander Jackson, Manuel Fullor and Cath-
erine Travis, the rest of our number are all well and
doing well. We are doing pretty well in the Agricultural line growing coffee, rice, sugar and we have no
right to complain of our situation it is true when we
first landed after the expiration of the six months
maintainance for the Society then we found it a little
difficult to do as well as we could wish yet we have
partially surmounted the difficulties and we are perfectly satisfied. We now are in the strictest sense of the
word Free. We have a church in our village where we
worship God and a school house where our children
are sent daily to receive instructions.

The individuals whose death I have mentioned
died in the triumps of faith and requested us to meet

them in heaven they left abright testimony behind them of being heirs to the Kingdom above.

You will please rember us to all acquaintances and especially to our colored friends and say to them that Liberia is the home for our race and as good a country as they can find. Industry and perserverance is only require to make a man happy and wealthy in this our Adopted Country, its soil yeilds abundant harvest to the husbandmon, its climate is healthy its laws are founded upon justice and equity here, we sit under our own vine and Palm Tree, we all enjoy the same rights and priviledges that our white brethren does in America it is our only home.

It has been some time since I received a letter from you I would be happy to hear from you at all times, with these few lines I close wishing God in his alwise providence to continue and bless you and all the friends in America and also to continue to extend his hands of care over us and at last bring us to live with him where parting no more shall be.

Respectfully yours &c.
Henrietta Fullor [7]

NOTES

PREFACE

[1] W. E. B. DuBois, preface, p. v, Herbert Aptheker, ed., *A Documentary History of the Negro People in the United States* (New York, 1951).

[2] Richard Hofstadter, "U. B. Phillips and the Plantation Legend," *Journal of Negro History* 29 (1944): 124.

[3] Kenneth M. Stampp, *The Peculiar Institution* (New York: Random House, 1956), pp. 88, 322.

[4] Stanley Elkins, *Slavery: A Problem in American Institutional and Intellectual Life* (Chicago: University of Chicago Press, 1959).

[5] George Fredrickson and Christopher Lasch, "Resistance to Slavery," *Civil War History* 13 (1967): 318–19, 324.

[6] Sterling Stuckey, "Through the Prism of Folklore: The Black Ethos in Slavery," *Massachusetts Review* 9 (1968): 417–37; Robert Ascher, "Excavation of a Georgia Slave Cabin," unpublished paper, Cornell University, Department of Archeology, 1969; Robert E. Thompson, "African Influence on the Arts of the United States," in Armstead L. Robinson et al., eds., *Black Studies in the University: A Symposium* (New Haven: Yale University Press, 1969), pp. 122–70.

[7] Gilbert Osofsky, ed., *Puttin' on Ole Massa: The Slave Narratives of*

Henry Bibb, William W. Brown, and Solomon Northrup (New York: Harper and Row, 1969); Julius Lester, ed., *To Be a Slave* (New York: Dell, 1968).

[8] Benjamin Drew, *North-Side View of Slavery—the Refugee: Or, the Narratives of Fugitive Slaves in Canada* (1856; reprint ed., New York: Johnson Reprint, 1969), is a useful collection of interviews.

[9] Though their texts are weak, Charles H. Nichols, *Many Thousand Gone: The Ex-Slaves' Account of Their Bondage and Freedom* (Bloomington, Ind.: Indiana University Press, 1969), and Margaret Y. Jackson, "An Investigation of Biographies and Autobiographies of American Slaves Published Between 1840 and 1860" (Ph.D. diss., Cornell University, 1954), both contain nearly complete lists of slave narratives. Cf. James B. Cade, "Out of the Mouths of Ex-Slaves," *Journal of Negro History* 22 (1935): 294–337; Fisk University, *God Struck Me Dead* (Nashville: Fisk University, 1945); George Rawick, *The American Slave: A Composite Autobiography* (8 vols.; Westport, Conn.: Negro Universities Press, 1970); and Julius Lester, ed., *To Be a Slave* (New York: Dell, 1968). Philip D. Curtin, ed., *Africa Remembered: Narratives of West Africans From the Era of Slave Trade* (Madison: University of Wisconsin Press, 1968), reprints and lists African narratives.

[10] Larry Gara, *The Liberty Line: The Legend of the Underground Railroad* (Lexington: University Press of Kentucky, 1961), pp. 122–23, discusses abolitionist ghostwriting and fictionalized slave narratives. Peter Neilson, ed., *The Life and Adventures of Zamba* (London, 1847), provides an extreme example of the problem of antislavery romanticism in a slave narrative, which is actually, according to Curtin, *Africa Remembered*, p. 6, a "blatant forgery." Charles Ball's *Life and Adventures* (New York, 1837), introduction, was admittedly "prepared by ——— Fisher from the verbal narrative of Ball." James Williams' *Narrative of an American Slave* (New York, 1838) was dictated to John Greenleaf Whittier by Williams.

[11] Benjamin A. Botkin, ed., *Lay My Burden Down: A Folk History of Slavery* (Chicago: University of Chicago Press, 1945); Federal Writers' Project, *Negro in Virginia* (New York, 1940); Julius Lester, *To Be a Slave* (New York: Dell, 1968).

[12] Edward P. Thompson, *The Making of the English Working Class* (New York: Pantheon, 1964); Eric J. Hobsbawm, *Primitive Rebels* (New

York: Norton, 1965): George Rude, *The Crowd in History, Seventeen Thirty to Eighteen Eighty-Four* (New York: Wiley, 1964); Jesse Lemisch, "Jack Tar in the Streets," *William and Mary Quarterly* 25 (1968): 371–407; Herbert G. Gutman, "The Worker's Search for Power: Labor in the Gilded Age," in H. Wayne Morgan, ed., *The Gilded Age* (Syracuse: Syracuse University Press, 1963), pp. 38–68.

[13] Jan Vansina, *The Oral Tradition: A Study in Historical Methodology* (Chicago: Aldine, 1965); Sterling Stuckey, "Through the Prism of Folklore: The Black Ethos in Slavery," *Massachusetts Review* 9 (1968): 417–37.

CHAPTER ONE

[1] From the Pettigrew Family Papers, Southern Historical Collection, University of North Carolina Library, Chapel Hill.

[2] Ibid.

[3] Ibid.

[4] Ibid.

[5] Ibid.

[6] Ibid.

[7] Ibid.

[8] Ibid.

[9] Ibid.

[10] Ibid.

[11] Ibid.

[12] Ibid.

[13] Ibid.

[14] Ibid.

[15] Ibid.

[16] Ibid.

[17] Ibid.

¹⁸ From the Pettigrew Family Papers, Southern Historical Collection, University of North Carolina Library, Chapel Hill.

¹⁹ Ibid.

²⁰ From the Tait Family Papers, Alabama State Department of Archives and History, Montgomery. Apparently dictated.

²¹ From the Andrew Brown Correspondence File, Learned Collection, Lumber Archives, University of Mississippi Archives, Oxford.

²² Ibid.

²³ Charles Colcock Jones, *Suggestions on the Religious Instruction of the Negroes in the Southern States* (1838; Philadelphia, 1947).

²⁴ From the Charles Colcock Jones Papers, Special Collections Division, Tulane University Library, New Orleans.

²⁵ Ibid. Probably dictated.

²⁶ Ibid. Probably dictated.

²⁷ Ibid. Probably dictated.

²⁸ Ibid. Probably dictated.

²⁹ Ibid. In his own hand.

³⁰ From the Historical Society of Pennsylvania, Philadelphia. In his own hand.

CHAPTER TWO

¹ From the David Campbell Papers, Duke University Library, Durham.

² Ibid.

³ Ibid.

⁴ Ibid.

⁵ From the DeRosset Family Papers, Southern Historical Collection, University of North Carolina Library, Chapel Hill. In his own hand.

[6] Ibid. In her own hand.

[7] Ibid. In his own hand.

[8] Ibid. In his own hand.

[9] Ibid. In his own hand.

CHAPTER THREE

[1] From the Ernest Haywood Collection, Southern Historical Collection, University of North Carolina Library, Chapel Hill.

[2] Ibid. In her own hand.

[3] From the Grinnan Papers, University of Virginia Library, Charlottesville. In his own hand.

[4] From the James Boon Papers, North Carolina State Archives, Raleigh. In her own hand.

[5] Ibid. Dictated.

[6] Ibid. In her own hand.

CHAPTER FOUR

[1] From the Miscellaneous Collection, New-York Historical Society, New York.

[2] *Journal of Negro History,* XIII (1928), 97–98.

[3] From the Pennsylvania Abolition Society Papers, Historical Society of Pennsylvania, Philadelphia.

[4] Ibid.

[5] Ibid. In his own hand.

[6] Ibid. In his own hand.

[7] From the American Colonization Society Papers, Library of Congress, Washington, D.C. In his own hand.

[8] Ibid.

[9] Ibid.

[10] Ibid.

[11] George M. Horton, *Poems By a Slave* (Philadelphia, 1837), pp. 7–8.

[12] Ibid., pp. 9–10.

[13] From the Neill Brown Papers, Duke University Library, Durham.

CHAPTER FIVE

[1] From the Otho Holland Williams Papers, Maryland Historical Society, Baltimore.

CHAPTER SIX

[1] *Calendar of Virginia State Papers* (18–18), IX, 147.

[2] Ibid., 150–151.

[3] Ibid., 159–160.

[4] Ibid., 154–156.

[5] Ibid., 171.

[6] Petition to the Virginia General Assembly, December 6, 1824, Legislative Papers, Virginia State Library, Richmond.

[7] Executive Papers, November 1812, Virginia State Library, Richmond.

CHAPTER SEVEN

[1] From the Joseph Long Papers, Duke University Library, Durham. In his own hand.

[2] From the Richard B. Riddick Papers, Duke University Library, Durham. In his own hand.

[3] Ibid. In his own hand.

[4] Ibid. In his own hand.

[5] From the Andrew Brown Correspondence File, Learned Collection, Lumber Archives, University of Mississippi, Oxford.

CHAPTER EIGHT

[1] From the American Colonization Society Papers, Library of Congress, Washington, D.C. In own hand.

[2] Ibid. In his own hand.

[3] Ibid. Dictated.

[4] Ibid. In his own hand.

[5] Ibid. In his own hand.

CHAPTER NINE

[1] From the John McDonogh Papers, Special Collections Division, Tulane University Library, New Orleans.

[2] Ibid.

[3] Ibid.

[4] From the John McDonogh Papers, Special Collections Division, Tulane University Library, New Orleans.

[5] Ibid.

[6] Ibid.

[7] Ibid.

ABOUT THE AUTHOR

ROBERT S. STAROBIN was born in New York City, received his B.A. from Cornell University, and his Ph.D. from the University of California, Berkeley. Until his death in 1971, he was a member of the History Department at the State University of New York at Binghamton. He was the author of *Industrial Slavery in the Old South* and the editor of *Denmark Vesey: The Slave Conspiracy of 1822*. *Blacks in Bondage* is the final work of a brilliant young historian of the American South.